From Research to I-Search

Creating Lifelong Learners for the 21st Century

By Lynn Bruno

ASSOCIATION FOR MIDDLE LEVEL EDUCATION
Westerville, Ohio

DEDICATION

Dedicated to all my students who never cease to amaze me!

ACKNOWLEDGEMENTS

I would like to thank my editor, Carla Weiland, whose unexpected invitation to write a book both thrilled me and scared me to death! Without her keen eye, talent, and expertise, it would have never happened. Nor would it have happened without the courage of the members of MiddleTalk who dare to raise the tough questions, fearlessly pursue the answers, and have for years challenged me to think deeply about my pedagogical practice. My journey with the I-Search paper would have never begun had my colleague, Jen Power, not directed me to Ken Macrories' original work when I came to doubt the value of traditional approaches to teaching research. In addition, I would be remiss if I did not also acknowledge the contributions made to this manuscript by two truly passionate and dedicated teachers, Ali Tannenbaum and Steve Wiemeler, who explored with me ways to adapt the I-Search process to accommodate time constraints faced by all classroom teachers. And of course, it goes without saying, I thank Bob, my husband, for his unflinching belief in me. However, my deepest gratitude goes to my students who challenge me everyday to become a better teacher by reminding me to be a good student.

Foreword

This book came into my life at exactly the time I needed it.

In my Humanities 7 course, my students design their own units together. They come up with massive tons of questions (hey, they're middle schoolers!), search for themes and connections, and watch as groups of questions begin to clump together and call out for their attention. Within each unit, we write a theme question to bring focus to our inquiry, choose two books, one for a read-aloud and one for a group read, design a number of group activities, and pursue and eventually share individually-chosen learning journeys including research, essay-writing, and presentations.

2 books

Over time, though, I found my students struggling with the research phase of the project. Some would quickly find a simple answer to their question and rest there, others would have no clue where to start, and still others would spend much more time following interesting but irrelevant tangents (a necessary if not altogether welcome byproduct of having access to the huge wealth of interconnected information that is the Internet) than investigating their actual question. This year, in a blatant and transparent attempt to maintain focus, I retitled the project their "Focus Question Essay." Intriguingly, while the quality of the Focus Questions themselves rose, the quality of research remained as random as ever. As my students began designing their second unit, I realized I needed some sort of technique to help guide them more specifically in their research so that the projects truly became a learning journey for all of them and not just a privileged few.

It was about that point in time that AMLE contacted me and asked me to write an introduction for this book. I had heard of I-Search papers before—from Lynn, through our interactions in listserves— but had inexplicably not taken the hint and run with the idea. This time, I was primed, and I sat down and devoured the book in one sitting. This is perhaps more a measure of my excitement than my perspicacity, as this is a book where each detail matters deeply. However, the potential of I-Search, as Lynn has thought it through and implemented it so effectively with her students, is enormous, and I have no doubt that my students, when they begin designing their next unit, will profit from the changes I will be incorporating.

Let's be very clear about this, then—Lynn Bruno is a master teacher. In taking us into not just her classroom but also her mind, she shows us an incredible array of factors that go into everything she does. I like to tell my students I usually have at least one good reason and often two or three for everything I do. With the design of, rationale for, and implementation of I-Search papers, Lynn makes me look like I'm winging it. Even better, she does so in a way that makes it utterly and completely accessible. And still better yet, she does so in a way that enables teachers to take her ideas and personalize them for their own classes, students, and styles. With all of this happening, I-Search becomes much more than an academic exercise. It becomes nothing less than a way to enable students to pursue their passions while learning and absorbing a multitude of skills and growing in knowledge, competence, and confidence.

Let your own learning journey begin.

Bill Ivey
Middle School Dean
Stoneleigh-Burnham School

Contents

Preface xi

FAQs about I-Search

1. Why are research skills important? 1
2. What is an I-Search paper? 1
3. What is the structure of the I-Search? 3
4. How does the I-Search relate to 21st century skills and lifelong learning? 4
5. How does the I-Search align with characteristics of the 21st century classroom? . . . 6
6. As a teacher, what does I-Search require of me? 7
7. How does I-Search relate to the Common Core State Standards? 7
8. What do I need to know about the Common Core literacy standards? 8
9. What do I need to know about teaching writing in all content areas? 10
10. I'm not a reading or writing teacher, so how can I teach these skills? 11
11. Can I-Search address the CCSS requirement for both short and
    long pieces of writing? 11
12. If I don't have time for assigning the whole process, can I still use the strategy? . . . 12
13. I have students with a wide range of abilities; can I differentiate
    using this strategy? 12
14. How should I evaluate the I-Search? 14
15. How would a team of teachers use this method? 15
16. Can all disciplines use the I-Search process? 15

Chapter 1   Planning an I-Search Unit 19

Chapter 2   What I Know/What I Want to Know 29

Lesson 1: Introducing I-Search 30
Lesson 2: Settling on a Topic: *What I Know* 34
Lesson 3: Setting the Pace and Scheduling 36
Lesson 4: Writing *What I Know* 38
Lesson 5: Discovering *What I Want to Know* 41
    Mini-lesson: How to analyze questions to narrow or broaden the topic 43

Chapter 3   The Research Journey 47

Lesson 6: Requirements, Format, and Models 48

Lesson 7: Finding Credible Sources 51

Lesson 8: Citations 53

Lesson 9: Conducting an Interview 54

Chapter 4   What I Learned 57

Lesson 10 Requirements and Format 58

Lesson 11 Writing a Thesis Statement 61

Lesson 12 Writing *What I Learned* 62

Lesson 13 Reflection 66

Chapter 5   We-Search and Other Time Savers .69

Chapter 6   More 21st Century Skills Strategies 79

Appendices

Appendix FAQ-1   The 21st Century Classroom. 85

Appendix 1-1   A Parent's Introduction to the I-Search Paper 87

Appendix 1-2   The 7 Domains of Lifelong Learning and I-Search 88

Appendix 1-3   CCSS Related to I-Search .89

Appendix 2-1   Finding a Researchable Topic 91

Appendix 2-2   Parent Letter and Topic Approval Form 92

Appendix 2-3   Cornell Notes 93

Appendix 2-4   Pacing Yourself Through the Project 94

Appendix 2-5   Scheduling the I-Search Project 95

Appendix 2-6   Student Checklist 96

Appendix 2-7   *What I Know* Standards-Based Rubric 97

Appendix 2-8   *What I Know* Self-Edit 99

Appendix 2-9   *What I Know* Peer-Edit 100

Appendix 2-10   Student Example of *What I Know* 101

Appendix 2-11   *What I Want to Know* Standards-Based Rubric 102

Appendix 2-12   *What I Want to Know* Self-Edit 104

Appendix 2-13   *What I Want to Know* Peer-Edit 105

Appendix 2-14   *Developing a Research Question* 106

Appendix 3-1 *Research Journey* Standards-Based Rubric 108

Appendix 3-2 *Research Journey* Self-Edit 112

Appendix 3-3 *Research Journey* Peer-Edit 114

Appendix 3-4 Example of *Research Journey* 116

Appendix 3-5 Website Evaluation Guide 118

Appendix 3-6 Whipping Up *Works Cited* 119

Appendix 3-7 The Art of Interviewing 120

Appendix 3-8 Interview Guide 122

Appendix 4-1 *What I Learned* Standards-Based Rubric 123

Appendix 4-2 *What I Learned* Self-Edit 126

Appendix 4-3 *What I Learned* Peer-Edit 127

Appendix 4-4 Summarizing and Synthesizing 128

Appendix 4-5 Key Phrases for Citing Evidence 128

Appendix 5-1 Presentation Software 129

Appendix 5-2 Presentation Rubric 131

References 133

Preface

video

The genesis of this book was a conversation that took place among middle level teachers in reaction to a video entitled *Teaching in the 21st Century*. From that conversation evolved a thoughtful discussion of the interplay between knowledge acquisition, learning theory, and pedagogical practice and how these elements impacted our ability to prepare our students for their future. It did not matter that each of the individuals involved in this conversation taught different content areas. The focus was how we evolve as educators to insure our students are equipped to succeed in a world that has yet to be. What role do we play in our students' learning? How much autonomy do we afford them in determining what and how they learn?

After reflecting on subsequent conversations of this professional learning community, I suggested that the I-Search unit was an example of the perfect marriage between a traditional approach to teaching and one that might better serve our students today given the world they will be inheriting. All teachers, regardless of their discipline, could use research, already a common instructional strategy of the PLC, to integrate 21st century skills into their teaching to prepare their students for success.

What I offered my colleagues was a shift in perspective. Rather than placing just one more thing on their plates, preparing our students for the 21st century was not adding to our curriculum, it asked us to adjust and shift our focus and perspective. By teaching the processes involved in learning and placing as much value on the mastery of those skills as teachers have historically placed on the products of learning, we can develop students' lifelong learning skills. Giving students more autonomy, not less; providing an environment in which all students are safe to take risks; where the learning process is valued, not the grade; these are the changes necessary if our students are to embrace the world in which they live. By adopting certain instructional changes to the process of research, all teachers, no matter what subject they teach, can begin to develop the lifelong learning skills their students will need.

FAQs about I-Search

1. Why are research skills important?

The ability to conduct research with fidelity is undeniably a life skill that not only benefits students when working for an academic grade, but in everyday decisions of varying degrees of importance. From something minor like choosing a new recipe for the evening's meal to more critical and life-determining decisions such as committing to a lifelong relationship, the ability to conduct reliable and purposeful research is an essential life skill upon which happiness is closely linked. The act of researching incorporates many skills that are required in the Common Core State Standards (CCSS) to raise the rigor of middle grades education to compete "in a twenty-first-century, globally competitive society" (2010, p. 3).

Throughout the process researching and writing the I-Search paper, students apply lifelong learning skills in authentic ways. The strategies, attitudes, skills, and processes required by the I-Search paper are universal and essential when engaging in a world filled with the unknown. Skills necessary for today's children to thrive and prosper in tomorrow's world are:

- To know the important questions to raise
- To know how to seek reliable sources that hold the answers
- To listen to others with an open mind
- To identify values and biases and consider alternative points of view
- To construct knowledge and develop understanding around big ideas
- To develop the confidence to add your voice to world conversations

If we as teachers are to prepare our students effectively, then teaching these skills is essential.

2. What is an I-Search paper?

A research process called I-Search was conceived by the late Ken Macrorie, who challenged the conventional hallmarks of writing instructions based on formulas and objectivity. Instead, he promoted recognizing the integral role of the writer's interests and experiences in good writing. *An I-Search paper differs from a traditional research paper in that valuing the writer's engagement with the content replaces the traditional value of remaining objective.* It recognizes the researcher's life context informs and shapes his or her opinions and the body of knowledge he or she constructs as a result of that research. The I-Search paper becomes a physical documentation of the act of researching, and the process has as much importance as the product. I-Search requires the researcher to identify what he or she already knows about the topic, what questions he or she would like answered, what knowledge others hold on the topic, and how that new knowledge has enriched and changed his or her understanding of the topic.

Some key elements of the I-Search are

- **Purpose.** Teachers focus on the cognitive processes students use to synthesize information and hold them accountable for communicating their thinking.

- **21st century skills.** Students demonstrate 21st century skills. They develop a critical curiosity about a topic, identify the relationships between events and ideas to develop a deeper meaning, open their minds to different perspectives, draw on learning relationships, monitor their strategies, and build their resilience.

- **Change in focus.** In schools, most assessments of research are based on the final written product—the research paper. As a result, students focus their energy on the writing of the paper, giving short shrift to the actual act of researching. The act of research often results in students skimming sources and working diligently to avoid plagiarism. The idea that research is about creating new knowledge by drawing from what others have learned is often lost in the pursuit of a grade.

  When I taught research in my literacy class, my 8th grade students went through the motions of researching a topic by focusing on the end result—unfortunately perceived by them to be roughly based on the 5-paragraph essay. They often took notes from one or two sources and rearranged the words in, more often than not, an unsuccessful attempt to avoid plagiarism. Both the students and I (in assessing them) saw this as a chore. There was no joy in the pursuit of knowledge, the discovery of answers, or the creation of new questions. In fact, there was rarely any evidence of something new being discovered, and most of the synthesis and analysis of information remained superficial.

- **Higher order skills.** Grouping by ideas rather than sources gives students valuable practice in synthesizing. Students learn that in a formal research paper, each paragraph is grouped by ideas as opposed to sources. At the middle school level, students tend to organize their writing around sources, much like they do in the Research Journey part of the I-Search paper. However, this does not promote the synthesis of information and how it changes understanding, the purpose of a research paper. By requiring a shift to grouping paragraphs by ideas at the end of the Research Journey, students are able to clearly see the difference between summarizing and synthesizing information. The What I Have Learned section, therefore, contains an introduction with a formally stated thesis, body paragraphs addressing that thesis and organized around big ideas, followed by a conclusion.

3. What is the structure of the I-Search?

Macrorie's outline of the I-Search paper reflected the actual process of research and provided a framework that placed the emphasis and value on the process of searching. As a college professor, he was not constrained by addressing the CCSS or the developmental needs of young adolescents. I adapted Macrorie's framework to address those needs but remained faithful to the purpose and goal—to teach students that it is the learning that is important.

Many young adolescents struggle with organization and pacing of their work and require assistance in structuring and planning longer pieces of writing. Chunking each section provided my students the opportunity to breakdown a complex assignment into manageable pieces. Perhaps more importantly, it provided the opportunity for my students to recognize the cognitive processes and corresponding actions needed to delve into a topic deeply enough to emerge in the end with new eyes. The framework that I use has been shaped by the feedback I have received from my students over the years and follows the following format:

1. **What I Know**—highlights the importance of background information, personal experiences, biases, and assumptions the student holds prior to conducting research. *The knowledge identified here does not need to be correct or accurate.* Realizing what false assumptions are held and how those assumptions can contribute to misunderstandings is essential to the learning process. This section satisfies the narrative element alluded to in the CCSS and that plays a critical piece in the development, analysis, and synthesis of knowledge. Unfortunately, what students think they know is a piece that often remains unknown to teachers, yet leads to misunderstandings and faulty assumptions.

2. **What I Want to Know**—the critical piece to the I-Search paper; the foundation on which all else is built. I spend a great deal of time walking my students through exercises designed to identify their curiosities and guiding them through the process of categorizing those curiosities into topics or disciplines that will both focus the student's research, while allowing for the breath of discovery. This is where students write the all-important guiding question from which they will later draft a thesis.

3. **Research Journey**—a review of the sources discovered during research; addresses skills of vetting sources, identifying how they found the sources, and determining criteria for their credibility. They then summarize the sources' information and the evidence used by the authors to support any conclusions. They conclude with a paragraph identifying how the knowledge in these sources has confirmed, challenged, supported, or altered their own understanding of the issue.

4. **What I Have Learned**—synthesis of information they have gathered. There are two options here. (1) In Ken Macrorie's I-Search paper, students continue to write this section in first person. I have followed this suggestion in the past with good results. This is a good option for teachers concentrating more on their content areas than fluidity in writing and parenthetical citations. (2) Due to the expectations of the high school with regard to writing, I have more recently required that the writing of this section reflect a formal research paper and shift from first person to third. This provides not only a wonderful opportunity to demonstrate how writing changes when shifting person, but also allows for the instruction of formal writing techniques such as academic transitions and parenthetical citations.

5. **Reflection**— Because reflecting on the process allows my students to identify the value of this process and an opportunity to share with me how to improve the process, I require a separate paragraph in which they share what they learned and what they found valuable and not so valuable during this unit of study.

6. **Works Cited**—I use the website EasyBib. Throughout the process students are counseled to input all sources they use into EasyBib so that this final step is easily accomplished by exporting their citations to a Word document. The biggest challenge is to develop the habit of securing a citation as a first step, not a last one.

4. How does the I-Search relate to 21st century skills and lifelong learning?

Dr. Ruth Deakin-Crick and her colleagues at the University of Bristol in England (Crick, Broadfoot, and Claxton, 2004) identified, condensed, and named seven domains of lifelong learning, all of which are embedded in an I-Search. I specifically teach students to be aware of those seven domains as they research so that they can strengthen their abilities in the areas in which they are weak. The seven domains and the areas each is practiced in I-Search are:

Domain 1. The *Changing and Learning* domain identifies an underlying belief system that is key in determining how individuals perceive their capacity to learn and change over time. What part do they believe their choices and actions play in their ability to learn? In other words, do they believe that learning is genetically predetermined, or do they feel that, no matter their heritage, through hard work, they can learn? A result of students' hard work on an I-Search paper is tangible evidence that they are capable of changing and learning and is identified in the reflection at the end of the process.

Domain 2. *Critical Curiosity* addresses the level of curiosity an individual holds toward learning new things and digging deeper into topics of interest. Does the student tend to ask questions directed toward developing a deeper understanding? How often does he or she independently research a topic of interest? This component of lifelong learning refers to an inherent drive to gain knowledge regardless of the presence of a material incentive (i.e., grade). In the I-Search process, identifying a research topic of great interest and maintaining that interest falls in this domain.

Domain 3. *Meaning Making* is a student's ability to anchor new concepts and ideas to known context in order to establish a broader and deeper foundational understanding on which to build knowledge and create new ideas. This is demonstrated by those students who instantly recognize the connectedness of the world; they readily connect ideas to events. They have a holistic approach to learning and tend not to departmentalize information, seeing relationships across content areas. In the What I Have Learned section of the I-Search paper, students describe how their research supports, changes, and expands the information they began with in the What I Know section of the paper.

Domain 4. *Creativity* refers to a student's ability to "think outside the box" rather than reference a talent for, say, music or art. In this case, creativity means a propensity for divergent thinking. Is the student playful enough in their learning to bend the rules? To explore the spaces between the given and the possible? In the I-Search process, synthesizing new information and forming new perspectives about their topic challenge students to think in creative ways.

Domain 5. *Resilience,* or the emotional response to difficulty in learning, provides strength for lifelong learning. Does a student react to challenges by internalizing them as personal failings, or does the student face the challenge and seize the opportunity to grow as a learner? The I-Search process is based on the fact that students lack information on a topic and must continually figure out what more there is to learn; it strengthens students' ability to identify and seek answers to questions.

Domain 6. *Strategic Awareness* addresses how reflective an individual is about his or her approach to learning. A strong lifelong learner develops the habit of not only determining the answer to questions, but also takes action to change strategies when it is evident that they are not yielding the desired results. A student with strong strategic awareness uses a multitude of approaches with intention. During the I-Search process, students follow specific time lines and processes for managing new information and constructing new knowledge.

Domain 7. *Learning Relationships* recognizes that learning occurs both in isolation and in community and that each contributes something invaluable to the process. To develop understandings, one needs time for independently processing information. Working through concepts, answering questions, and solving problems in the safety of one's own company is essential to learning. At the same time, working with others and hearing their interpretations and perceptions helps to expand and broaden personal knowledge by providing alternative lenses through which to see. Knowing when each is needed and how each enriches learning is key to becoming a strong lifelong learner. In the I-Search process, students learn how critical this domain is to research as they peer-edit, interview experts, and request assistance from the teacher, librarian, and technology specialist.

By purposefully developing pedagogy designed to strengthen and develop strong learning profiles for our students, educators can create learner-centered classrooms built on relevant curriculum that simultaneously delivers meaningful content while it creates robust lifelong learners fully prepared to succeed in the 21st century.

5. How does the I-Search strategy align with characteristics of the 21st century classroom?

A 21st century classroom rests on three core foundational principals: authenticity, autonomy, and time. Ask anyone what factors were present when they think back on a lesson learned well, and chances are, these three elements were present.

Authentic learning is learning that occurs while doing meaningful work. When students engage in work that piques their interest and holds a specific purpose that is valued, then the learning in authentic. Although students need not immediately realize the value of their learning, they must be convinced that the knowledge they are seeking is essential. That requires the teacher's ability to identify the applicability of the knowledge to life and the student's ability to see the possibilities that the future holds, no easy task, for sure. However, there is no doubt that we learn best when we can see a useful application of the knowledge in our own lives and the work or skills involved are connected to an authentic need to know.

Autonomy. Critical to understanding is *autonomy* in learning, and it is best expressed through the domain of Meaning Making. Autonomy is the ability to develop a broader and deeper understanding of a topic by building on past experience and knowledge. If we have the autonomy to make our own choices in how we learn, and whenever possible, what we learn, we are able to take ownership of that learning and draw from and build on what we already know. In so doing, we become personally invested. The child and his or her personal intellectual, psychological, and sociological experiences are critical to the learning. The ultimate goal of the teacher in the 21st century remains the same as those teachers that came before—to guide their students toward becoming fully participatory and engaged citizens, capable of debating complex issues and making decisions for the good of all (Brown, 2006; Mondale and Patton, 2001; Springer, 2006).

Time. But, perhaps the most important aspect of learning something well is the time to do so. It is, arguably, the most difficult piece to provide students because time is finite. However, effective and valuable learning occurs when students have enough time to research, learn, process, create, and apply their newfound knowledge. Maurice Holt, in his 2002 article, *It's Time To Start The Slow School Movement,* likens the narrowing of the curriculum and the 'drill and kill' focus on reading and math prompted by the NCLB legislation to fast food dining. He calls for opponents to adopt the same approach of the slow food movement used in France in reaction to the growing presence of fast food restaurants. Holt argues that if life is getting more complex, then it is important that we create educational experiences that develop a student's ability to explore complex issues. The current trend to focus solely on product is counterproductive. Holt calls for what he refers to as the slow school, "…where understanding matters more than coverage." It is only by providing students and teachers the space for scrutiny, argument, and resolution that we will adequately prepare students of today for tomorrow.

Appendix FAQ-1 details the characteristics of the 21st century classroom—function, physical setting, teacher-student relationship, and the role of students.

6. As a teacher, what does I-Search require of me?

In addition to providing an environment in which students feel safe taking risks, the I-Search asks for a change in teacher perspective and adjustment of focus. Instead of the paper (product) having the major emphasis (and therefore, value), the process of research and students' awareness of their moving through it are just as important.

If the seven domains of lifelong learning are taught to students, teachers and students will benefit. Once students know their strengths and weaknesses, they can decide where to target their efforts for improvement, and teachers can more accurately direct instructional practice and assist students in developing these attributes and skills. Process, then, becomes as important as product. Teachers must not only develop lessons designed to teach content, but also consider the necessary pedagogical practices that develop and strengthen lifelong learning.

7. How does the I-Search relate to the Common Core State Standards?

Although the CCSS are dense and complex, they attempt to address the value of incorporating goals for lifelong learning into students' process of acquiring content knowledge, and I-Search is a strategy that gives students opportunities to demonstrate their level of belief in their ability to change and learn, engage their critical curiosity, creativity, and meaning making as well as employ learning relationships in order to reach mastery. I-Search is hard work, and requires students to develop and refine their strategic awareness and potentially, their resilience. For me, the CCSS places learning into authentic action, and by avoiding a checklist approach, requires teachers to abandon a traditional conception of teacher as the all-knowing sage on stage and move to the role of co-learner and coach. In so doing, students are given the freedom to discover knowledge and hone their skills through authentic work. They are given the opportunity to develop into lifelong learners.

The good news is that none of these standards occur in isolation. The reading and writing standards are not designed as a checklist of behavioral skills that can be addressed in isolation. Rather, they describe cognitive and physical behaviors that are synchronized and occur seamlessly.

8. What do I need to know about the Common Core literacy standards?

Although some content teachers perceive this expectation as "just one more thing" added to an already full curriculum, the reasoning behind the standards is sound. According to the CCSS, the justification for requiring the teaching of reading in all content areas is:

> Reading is critical to building knowledge in history/social studies as well as in science and technical subjects. College and career ready reading in these fields requires an appreciation of the norms and conventions of each discipline, such as the kinds of evidence used in history and science; an understanding of domain-specific words and phrases; an attention to precise details; and the capacity to evaluate intricate arguments, synthesize complex information, and follow detailed descriptions of events and concepts. In history/social studies, for example, students need to be able to analyze, evaluate, and differentiate primary and secondary sources. When reading scientific and technical texts, students need to be able to gain knowledge from challenging texts that often make extensive use of elaborate diagrams and data to convey information and illustrate concepts. Students must be able to read complex informational texts in these fields with independence and confidence because the vast majority of reading in college and workforce training programs will be sophisticated nonfiction. It is important to note that these reading standards are meant to complement the specific content demands of the disciplines, not replace them (60).

CCSS adds focus on process. There is no doubt that content area teachers have been teaching these cognitive skills for years. No matter the curricular area, the ability to evaluate and synthesize complex information is necessary to establish a deep understanding of the issues presented in any discipline. The standards for reading imposed onto content area teachers does not, in reality, add to the curricular content. It does, however, bring to the forefront the need for teachers to focus on teaching their students the cognitive processes needed to access and analyze critical information as opposed to their ability to simply regurgitate that knowledge. Figure FAQ-1 details the relationship of I-Search to 21st century skills and the CCSS.

Figure FAQ-1: *Comparison of I-Search to 21st century skills and CCSS*

Relationship of I-Search to 21st century skills and CCSS

Research/ 21st century skills	Where in I-Search?	Where in CCSS?
Citing evidence	Research Journey; What I Learned; Works Cited	Reading Informational Text: RI-8.1; RI-8.2; RI-8.3; RI-8.4; RI-8.6; RI-8.9; Writing W-8.2, W-8.2a-f; W-8.4; W-8.5; W-8.7; W-8.8
Reasoned, logical demonstration of position	What I Know; What I Want to Know; Research Journey; What I Learned	Reading Informational Text: RI-8.1; RI-8.2; RI-8.3; RI-8.4; RI-8.6 Writing W-8.2, W-8.2a-f; W-8.3; W-8.3a-e; W-8.4; W-8.5; W-8.7; W-8.8
Synthesizing	What I Know; What I Want to Know; What I Learned	Reading Informational Text: RI-8.1; RI-8.9 Writing W-8.2; W-8.2a-f; W-8.3; W-8.3a-e; W-8.4; W-8.5; W-8.7; W-8.8
Communicating thinking	What I Know; What I Want to Know; Research Journey; What I Learned	Reading Informational Text: RI-8.1; RI-8.2; RI-8.3; RI-8.4; RI-8.6 Writing W-8.2, W-8.2a-f; W-8.3; W-8.3a-e; W-8.4; W-8.5; W-8.7; W-8.8
Accurately conveys information	What I Know; Research Journey; What I Learned; Works Cited	Reading Informational Text: RI-8.1; RI-8.2; RI-8.3; RI-8.4; RI-8.6 Writing W-8.2, W-8.2a-f; W-8.3; W-8.3a-e; W-8.4; W-8.5; W-8.7; W-8.8

9. What do I need to know about teaching writing in all content areas?

New writing expectations will take time from classes. With regard to writing, the expectation may not necessarily add content to the social studies, science, and technical curriculums, but there is no doubt it will require more class time. The time it takes to write coherently and effectively and to assess that writing is extensive. However, the genres of writing that are addressed in the content areas are informative and argumentative. These genres emphasize logical reasoning and relevant evidence used to examine and/or convey complex ideas and information. Again, the focus is on the cognitive process used to synthesize various sources of information and effectively present that information in an organized and coherent manner. Notice, grammar is not addressed in the standards assigned to content area teachers. Note, that while narrative writing is listed as a genre, this expectation simply requires "that students be able to incorporate narrative elements effectively into argumentative and informative/explanatory texts" (65). In the content disciplines, the overwhelming focus is for students to demonstrate the ability to communicate their analysis, ideas, and conclusions in writing. According to the CCSS, the justification for holding all teachers to writing standards is:

> For students, writing is a key means of asserting and defending claims, showing what they know about a subject, and conveying what they have experienced, imagined, thought, and felt. To be college and career ready writers, students must take task, purpose, and audience into careful consideration, choosing words, information, structures, and formats deliberately. They need to be able to use technology strategically when creating, refining, and collaborating on writing. They have to become adept at gathering information, evaluating sources, and citing material accurately, reporting findings from their research and analysis of sources in a clear and cogent manner. They must have the flexibility, concentration, and fluency to produce high-quality first draft text under a tight deadline and the capacity to revisit and make improvements to a piece of writing over multiple drafts when circumstances encourage or require it. To meet these goals, students must devote significant time and effort to writing, producing numerous pieces over short and long time frames throughout the year (63).

Teaching writing across disciplines is imperative if students are to become adept at communicating. By requiring students to author a variety of writing genres, from short responses under timed conditions to longer pieces with less arduous time restraints, educators prepare their students to meet the demands placed on them in both academia and the workforce. It is evident that the CCSS has placed the onus on all teachers to move beyond the accumulation of basic knowledge and teach their students to communicate that knowledge in authentic ways.

10. I'm not a reading or writing teacher, so how can I teach these skills?

I recognize that writing is a difficult process. Given the complexity of the English language and the seemingly endless number of rules, not to mention the exceptions to those rules, the act of writing can be daunting to everyone, especially students. As a literacy teacher, I am expected to know all of them, and yet I freely admit I do not. My students receive this information with a mixture of disbelief and awe, but it is essential that students understand that not knowing something does not equate to failure, but rather an opportunity to learn. I share with my students my own challenges with writing, and when there is a question I cannot answer, we seek the answer together. In doing so, I model resilience and the power of learning relationships.

As Jill Spencer says in *10 Differentiation Strategies for Building Common Core Literacy* (2013)

> We need to **model the "growth mindset"** in everything we do with students, including in helping them become highly skilled readers and writers. For example, when facing a grammar issue, it's OK to say, "I'm not really sure where that comma should go in this compound sentence—let's see what Grammar Girl has to say!" (http://grammar.quickanddirtytips. com/) Or, "This is a complex piece on DNA; let's put it up on the Smart Board and work through it together." By demonstrating to students how we solve problems we face while reading and writing, we set an example for students to emulate. Not giving up when faced with stumbling blocks and learning specific strategies to use will help build their academic resiliency.

The insecurity that some content teachers may harbor concerning their lack of expertise in teaching reading and writing is not unlike the concerns felt by literacy teachers when collaborating with content area teachers. During a cross-curricular unit of study one year, my science colleague and I co-taught the teaching of a research paper in which I instructed the students in reading writing and assessed the paper for writing while he instructed them in the scientific concepts and assessed the papers for content. The papers addressed a subject I was unfamiliar with and he had no confidence in teaching writing, yet during the process both he and I modeled the joy of learning something we previously did not know, and we did it visibly so that our students could benefit. Becoming co-learners with your students is one of the strongest lessons teachers can offer in lifelong learning.

11. Can I-Search address the CCSS requirement for both short and long pieces of writing?

Because the CCSS specifically requires both short and long pieces of writing, an I-Search, by chunking the writing into manageable pieces, meets this expectation and covers all the required reading and writing standards while building learning capacity through the seven domains of lifelong learning.

Teaching writing across disciplines is imperative if students are to become adept at communicating. By requiring students to author a variety of writing genres, from short responses under timed conditions to longer pieces with less arduous time restraints, educators prepare their students to meet the demands placed on them in both academia and the workforce. It is evident that the CCSS has placed the onus on all teachers to move beyond the accumulation of basic knowledge and teach their students to communicate that knowledge in authentic ways.

12. If I don't have time for assigning the whole process, can I still use the strategy?

While the time invested in this unit may seem prohibitive, the rapid improvement in skills afforded the student by the opportunity to immerse themselves in their work is quite remarkable and worth the time invested. The I-Search paper addresses a multitude of standards, and some are addressed several times.

However, content area teachers may not be able to invest 6 weeks on one unit, 7 to 8 if you include the presentation of findings; this is an enormous amount of time for content area teachers, who in addition to the reading and writing standards established by the CCSS, have specific content standards to meet. See Chapter 5 for suggestions for doing the I-Search process with fewer drafts, fewer sections, as part of a teaching team, and with alternate products—strategies that significantly reduce the amount of time required.

13. I have students with a wide range of abilities; can I differentiate using this strategy?

The I-Search paper is designed to provide every learner the opportunity to succeed. It is focused on the process as opposed to the product, and so students experience successes throughout, helping to build their confidence by recognizing the knowledge they have gained along the way. This helps to build the domain of Changing and Learning as well as Resilience. Because it involves a mix of writing genres and choice in the sources used, students at all levels can achieve. For those students who struggle with writing formal papers, the ability to structure their paper informally allows them to more accurately share their journey. Accessing resources at their reading level allows struggling readers to gain the content knowledge they seek. The level of expectations can be individualized to challenge students while insuring their success. Some suggestions for modifying the I-Search to accommodate struggling learners include:

- Graphic organizers, storyboarding, annotation of text
- Student support groups that share strategies that have worked
- Providing models and schedules accompanied with reminders
- Posting of upcoming due dates on board/websites/emails
- Scaffolding the project using the Gradual Release of Responsibility model:
  1. I do—teacher models
  2. We do it together.
  3. You do it independently.

Other strategies that are helpful in addressing the variety of learning levels found in evey classroom might include the following:

a. Encourage students reading at or above grade level to use more complex texts and sources and ask more complex or nuanced questions;

b. Build the confidence of more struggling readers by supporting them in finding materials they will find highly engaging.

c. Select Read Alouds on the topics struggling readers have selected for their I-Search. This allows for their classmates to model the metacognitive processes used to interpret and analyze text.

d. Push all students to clarify their thoughts and stretch their understanding of ideas in conferences.

e. Develop go-to teams consisting of 3 to 4 students. This provides a steady source of support for students while at the same time strengthening the domain of learning relationships and strategic awareness.

f. Use small group instruction to work on specific challenges to effectively target the learning needs of individual students.

g. Use assistive technology software if it is available at your school to help students with hearing and vision impairments or fine motor issues to be more successful. Some of the software is built into computers and tablets, and some has to be purchased. Adaptations include flashes instead of sounds for alerts, font size changes, background color changes, text-to-speech and speech-to-text capabilities, and change of keyboard language.

h. ELL students can write in their native languages using various translation sites to formulate and organize ideas.

Alternate products: Allowing students to synthesize their learning in alternate formats that highlight their strengths can allow for the assessment of critical thinking and understandings. There are strategies that teachers can adopt to not only streamline the I-Search process, but also address a variety of learning challenges. The synthesizing of what has been learned can be presented in a variety of text and media formats. Some examples are:

- oral presentations with graphics
- panel discussions
- debates
- design and building of a model
- visual representation (graphic novel, painting, poster,)
- digital presentation
- leading a virtual field trip
- design and implementation of a simulation
- dramatic presentation
- textbook chapter

Although students will be assessed by the state on written essays and not alternative products, the Common Core literacy standards involve building arguments, developing informational text, and creating narratives. Offering alternative products as a choice for students allows them to practice the critical thinking processes involved in writing the traditional essays and narratives and can address the Common Core Standards for Reading Informational Text.

14. How should I evaluate the I-Search?

You will find rubrics in the Appendix that help students meet standards by clearly stating the criteria for acceptable and exemplary work. In addition, there are self- and peer-edit sheets that are directly linked to the rubrics and emphasize content and organization. At the middle school level, students tend to believe that editing means simply correcting conventions and spelling. It is important that students develop the habit of focusing on substance and form when beginning to draft their writing. A polish edit prior to submission can catch errors in convention, but until the paper communicates important information in a way that promotes understanding, fixating on conventions is ineffective. Distribute both the self- and peer-edit sheets and the rubric prior to the start of a section, and use models of former students' work as you review these with students.

Before submission, students should self assess their work using the rubric. Because students often rush to assess their work once it is completed, Jill Spencer (2013) offers the suggestion of getting students to slow down and thoughtfully use rubrics:

Ask them to highlight evidence in their draft of where they have met the criteria.

i. *Use strong and/or technical vocabulary*—highlight 6 examples.

ii. *Use statistics as one type of evidence*—highlight your statistics and your citation.

iii. *Use varied sentence structure*—highlight 3 different types of sentences in our piece.

The highlighting (or lack thereof) provides visual cues to the student of where they need to revise the content; these concrete guideposts tell the reluctant writer what to do next. (p. 138)

Having students assess their work begins the process of shifting the value of a teacher's perspective back to their own. Years of schooling have taught students that their teachers are the only ones who can determine the value of their work. If students are to become strong lifelong learners, they need to develop confidence in their ability to assess the value of their own work. Providing the opportunity to do so and requiring them to identify the evidence to support their assessment strengthens their ability to think critically.

15. How would a team of teachers use this method?

A team approach to the I-Search paper has a multitude of benefits, not the least of which is a distribution of the workload in assessing student work. The development of an I-Search project could be designed within a PLC to address multiple standards and would most likely take on the elements of project-based learning. By identifying broad essential questions, teams could preserve the element of choice so integral to the success of the I-Search paper, allowing students the flexibility to pursue their personal interest within the parameters set by the question. For example, essential questions such as, *"When is it appropriate to challenge the beliefs or values of a society?"* would allow students with a strong interest in the sciences to pursue ethical questions raised by scientific research such as the use of stem cells or cloning, while those students interested more in the social science might pursue research addressing human rights or governance.

Lawrence Middle School on Long Island, interdisciplinary teams of 7th grade teachers follow a 4-phase model based on theme. During Phase I, Teachers engage students in authentic activities related to a theme such as a socially relevant topic linking science, social studies, language arts, and math (the human body, the environment, impact of technology on society). During Phase II, students develop their own search plans, based on their guiding question Moving into Phase III, students delve into the research, revising their search plan if necessary and gather the information they need to answer their questions. Finally, in Phase IV, students organize their information in writing in preparation for the presentation of that information through a variety of options (Zorfass & Copel, 2000).

16. Can all disciplines use the I-Search process?

Yes! Perhaps the best way to determine a topic for I-Search is to mine the minds of your students. Ask the students what really interests them. Teachers can help to model meaning making by taking ideas and bridging them to current events or current curriculum foci. By looking at the breadth of the topics in which students hold an interest, essential questions or themes can be tailored to address those interests. Once a theme or essential question is identified, providing students access to resources to learn and explore can help them to narrow their interest. By providing a list of websites or a plethora of magazines or books to meander through, students can discover issues that are related to their interest, but were perhaps formerly unknown. For example, I gave my students the following chart based on the theme "Tikum Olam" (Repair the World) and on a discussion of topics that interested them; they explored each of these organizations to determine if any sparked a passion to know more.

Organizations and People to Explore Based on "Tikkun Olam"

Organizations	People
Peace Jam: http://www.peacejam.org/meet_laureates.htm	Abudacar Sultan – Child Soldiers (Mozambique)
Free the Children: http://www.freethechildren.com/index.php	Bruce Harris – Homeless Children's Rights / Street Kids (Central America)
Peace Corp: http://www.peacecorps.gov/	Muhammad Yunus – MicroCredit (Bangladesh)
Youth Action International: http://www.peaceforkids.org/	Rana Husseini – Honor Killings (Jordan)
Amnesty International Canada: www.amnesty.ca	The Dalai Lama – Religious Freedom (Tibet)
Doctors Without Borders: www.doctorswithoutborders.org	Wangari Maathai – Women and the Environment (Kenya)
Human Right Watch: http://www.hrw.org/	Oscar Arias Sanchez – Disarmament (Costa Rica)
Greenpeace: http://www.greenpeace.org/usa/	Dianna Ortiz – Torture (Guatemala/United States)
Child Labor Public Education Project http://www.continuetolearn.uiowa.edu/laborctr/child_labor/	Hafez Al Sayed Seada – Political Rights (Egypt)
Sweatshop Free Communities http://www.sweatfree.org/organizations#solidarityorgs	Desmond Tutu – Reconciliation (South Africa)
Red Cross:(Human Rights) http://www.redcross.org	Senal Sarihan – Political Rights (Turkey)
United Nations: (Human Rights) http://www.un.org/en/rights/index.shtml	Van Jones – Police Brutality (United States)
AFL/CIO: (Workers' Rights/ Sweatshops) http://www.aflcio.org/corporatewatch/stop/	Ka Hsaw Wa – Multinational Corporate Responsibility (Burma)
People for the Ethical Treatment of Animals: http://www.peta.org/	Juan Mendez – Human Rights and Reconciliation (Argentina)

National Coalition against Domestic Violence: http://www.ncadv.org/	Jaime Prieto Mendez – Political Rights (Colombia)
Prevent Child Abuse America - http://www.preventchildabuse.org/index.shtml	Bobby Muller – (International Ban on Land Mines) United States
Child Soldiers http://www.child-soldiers.org/home	Raji Sourani – Human Rights and Self-Determination (Gaza)
The Holocaust http://www.ushmm.org/wlc/en/article.php?ModuleId=10005143	Doan Viet Hoat – Political Rights and Imprisonment (Vietnam)
Human Trafficking - http://www.humantrafficking.org/	Natasa Kandic – Human Rights in Time of War (Serbia) Elie Wiesel – The Powerless (Romania/United States - Holocaust) Maria Teresa Tula – the Disappeared (El Salvador) Rigoberta Menchu Tum – Indigenous Peoples' Rights (Guatemala) Marian Wright Edelman – Children and Poverty (United Sates) Helen Prejean – The Death Penalty (United States) Patria Jimenez – Gay, Lesbian, and Transgender Rights (Mexica) Marina Pisklakova – Domestic Violence (Russia) Harry Wu – The Laogai - Prison Labor - (China)

Planning an I-Search Unit

Take time to deliberate, but when the time for action comes, stop thinking and go in.
—Napoleon Bonaparte

Designing a unit of study in any discipline involves considering content objectives, learning needs of students, state standards, and the time available. Although the amount of work involved can feel prohibitive, time invested prior to the implementation of any unit of study is well spent, and taking a proactive approach to insure student and parent support will pay dividends far in excess of time invested.

The unit discipline's cognitive concepts and skills become the objectives, and now that the CCSS require all teachers to teach critical reading and effective writing, some of the objectives related to critical reading and effective writing will be shared across the curriculum.

Traditionally, teachers write content objectives in behavioral terms that are observable and measurable. However, lifelong learning goals are not so easily identified in behavioral terms. Articulating how each of the seven domains is woven into various aspects of the I-Search unit assists students in developing the strategies they need to become effective and successful lifelong learners and will often result in higher performance on the content-based objectives.

The planning of any unit should begin by asking the seemingly simple question, "Why?" If the answer to the common student-generated inquiry, "Why do we need to know this?" identifies something of personal value in the content or process, the work becomes authentic to students. As a result they will take ownership, engage willingly, and, when the work becomes difficult, they will persevere.

It's important to remain flexible and reflective throughout the planning and implementation of any unit because as more and more is learned, the objectives, the rationale, and how lifelong learning is supported may shift to meet the specific needs of current students, freeing the teacher to incorporate new technologies and understandings. However, for the purpose of clarity, in this chapter, each component will be addressed separately.

Writing Content-Based Objectives

When developing the I-Search unit, identifying the content-based objectives that will be taught is critical. In many disciplines, the topic of research will be dictated by the particular concepts or content students are learning. The more latitude a student has in selecting the topic of research, the more invested the student will be in the process. Because choice and personal interest are at the core of meaningful and effective learning and my discipline allows for an umbrella theme, I use "Tikkun olam," a Hebrew phrase that means "Repair the World." My students identify a topic of research connected to world issues related to any discipline that interests them. They have researched a wide variety of topics ranging from human rights violations including research on child labor and human trafficking, health issues such as eating disorders and obesity, and environmental issues such as global warming and access to drinkable water, just to name a few.

Once you determine a theme, you can identify the content-based objectives. Because the CCSS requires the same standards for reading and writing in the content areas as are required in literacy, many of the objectives I list for my unit of study are universal and usable in a variety of disciplines. When I began identifying objectives for this unit of study, I found it helpful to consider each section of the I-Search paper separately. My list of content-based objectives is based on my overarching theme and grounded in my discipline.

Figure 1-1: *Example of unit objectives*

"Tikkun olam."
I-Search Unit: Objectives

1. To demonstrate the ability to choose a researchable topic, one that is neither too broad nor too narrow, and is related to the established theme.

2. To develop a focused research question and use that question to frame and direct the research.

3. To illustrate the metaconitive processes that are used during research by demonstrating the ability to:

   a. Identify and communicate background knowledge of the topic.

   b. Apply the criteria needed to determine if a topic is researchable.

   c. Construct reasonable questions designed to get to the heart of the answers being sought.

   d. Demonstrate the ability to sort information into manageable categories (i.e. social, political, economic, etc.)

   e. Develop a well-structured guiding question to frame the research.

   f. Incorporate new, researchable questions into the research as more information is discovered.

   g. Demonstrate the ability to identify a variety of sources from which answers to questions may appear, including, but not limited to:

      i. Internet search engines and the use of key words

      ii. Library/Media sources (the value of a good librarian)

      iii. Individuals as resources (who do you know?)

      iv. Organizational resources (what organizations/community groups can help?)

   h. To critically read and annotate sources in search of answers to questions.

   i. To identify and learn new and challenging vocabulary that is discovered during the research process.

   j. To share in the writing personal thoughts and feelings, highlighting any shift in thinking throughout the research process as perspective broadens and knowledge expands.

4. To summarize the information in each source and demonstrate an ability to do so without plagiarizing.

5. To identify the information necessary to construct a citation for each source according to MLA or APA style.

6. To synthesize the new knowledge with the old knowledge and be able to express how the research process has changed perspective and/or opened new paths of inquiry.

7. To support the argument with valid evidence for why this topic is of importance and related to the assigned theme.

8. To effectively use parenthetical citations.

9. To effectively use academic transitions.

10. To produce clear and coherent writing in which the development of ideas, organization, word choice, and voice engage and educate the reader.

11. With regard to self and peer-editing:

   a. To demonstrate thoughtful critical and respectful analysis of classmates' work.

   b. To demonstrate the ability to engage in an inquiry-based conversation with others.

   c. To share new knowledge with other members of the learning community that might assist them in their research journey.

Articulating the Rationale

I believe the most crucial element of unit design is articulating the rationale for my choices of content objectives and how those objectives will be met. Doing so before implementing the unit of study has several benefits. For a lengthy unit involving student discovery, articulating the rationale upfront provides transparency as well as a framework to keep students and teacher focused. Taking the time to write the rationale for why you have chosen to frame this lesson in this way provides the educator the opportunity to insure that the learning is authentic and meaningful. By articulating the importance and value of the unit of study beforehand, teachers are able to provide a well-thought-out and articulate response to students who question the value of the exercise. Additionally, on those rare occasions when a student, parent, or administrator questions the purpose of a unit, I am able to address with confidence their concerns.

I begin the process of writing a rationale by simply listing the reasons I have identified as a need either for inclusion or change in the curriculum. In addition, I incorporate into that list what I have come to learn about my specific students and their needs. My rationale for moving from a research paper to an I-Search paper began by identifying why I felt a change was needed in how the teaching of research was traditionally approached in literacy. The realization that a change was needed came from my students; their learning needs as well as their perceptions of and attitudes towards research. When I took time to reflect on how I could better serve the needs of my students, I was able to identify the answers to the question, "Why?" Figure 1-2 is an example of a rationale for changing from traditional research to I-Search.

Figure 1-2: *Example of rationale for changing from traditional research to I-Search*

Rationale for I-Search rather than Research

1. Most formal writings require the writer to draw from their background knowledge and experience in addition to doing some, if not a great deal, of research in order to inform or persuade.

2. Most 8th grade students rush through the research process, relying largely on background knowledge and experience, with a focus on the final product, losing sight of the importance and the power of the research journey.

3. Traditional research papers are focused on writing. The I-Search paper focuses largely on the research process and reinforces the steps all good research requires, building strong lifelong learning skills in the process.

4. The I-Search paper is a visual representation of the process that individuals go through when they want to learn more about a topic, providing tangible evidence of the metacognitive processes that are involved in research.

5. Because most sections are written in 1st person, the contribution of the individual's background knowledge and experience as it relates to interpretation and understanding is revealed and valued. This reveals the context and origin of the students' understanding as well as the conclusions they draw.

6. Chunking the assignment into manageable pieces teaches students not only to understand the important role of all aspects of research, but also gives them instruction in how to break down and manage larger projects.

Communicating with Parents

This list serves to answer the "Why" questions that students may raise and is the basis for a written rationale that takes on the form of a parent letter (see Appendix 1-1). In that letter, I explain the project and its rationale. This serves the dual purpose of providing parents with a brief description of the project expectations and gives them information to use when their son or daughter comes to them with questions or complaints. Informative, yet friendly in tone, the letter helps build a cooperative relationship with parents. In addition to emailing the letter, I send home hard copies and post it on my website.

Providing a rationale to my parents, results in a multitude of benefits for all stakeholders. Throughout the unit, parents or guardians will be asked to assist their child in different ways, and this letter serves to give them the foundational understanding needed in order to best provide that support. Because of the length and complexity of the unit, it often triggers a response from a parent about organizational issues their child has, and together, we develop a plan to help that child succeed. In addition, when the time comes for the interviews, parents often volunteer to be available to interview on a topic in which they have some expertise. I can't overstate the value of articulating a rationale.

Incorporating Lifelong Learning

Not only do I want my students to know how to read and write effectively, I want them to build their learning confidence so that they are capable of meeting new challenges in the future. At the beginning of the year, I discuss the seven domains of lifelong learning with students and they have a pretty good sense of where their strengths and weaknesses lie. When planning any unit of study, I list not only the content knowledge and skills required by my discipline, I also consider how each of the seven domains of lifelong learning are manifested. By sharing with my students where in the process they will lean on their critical curiosity or their creativity, for example, I help to make more tangible the behaviors and dispositions that inform and strengthen learning. This enables students who wish to strengthen a particular domain to target specific steps in the process and apply strategies that will help them grow in that area. It also assists me as a teacher by identifying where during the process I need to be attentive to certain students who need support to strengthen their learning profile. By doing so, my students are able to identify their personal learning goals for the I-Search paper. The student handout explaining how 21st century skills are connected to their work on the I-Search paper is located in Appendix 1-2, "The 7 Domains of Lifelong Learning and I-Search".

Taking the time to help students visualize the seven domains of lifelong learning within the context of the unit plan provides them the opportunity to strengthen their learning profile and alerts me to points at which my guidance and support may be needed. While the rubrics will provide an assessment of their finished work, the opportunity to set a personal goal for their own learning and have tangible proof of meeting that goal is powerful. I have my students identify which of the seven domains of lifelong learning they feel they need to strengthen, and throughout the project we identify evidence that indicates growth in those domains. When faced with a particular challenge, I am able to suggest strategies designed to strengthen those domains.

Mapping a Plan

Once you establish the objectives and rationale, the next step is to map out the unit of study on a calendar. The amount of time dedicated to this unit plan is determined by a number of factors—the objectives and standards identified, the skills and needs of the students, the demands of a particular curriculum, the school's schedule, and the requirements.

A. Identify requirements and specific lessons. I begin the unit scheduling by identifying the requirements specific to my discipline and informed by my rationale. Because it is dependent on so many variables, this list is unique to each teacher. Establishing the requirements will also help to highlight any particular lessons that may be necessary for students to succeed. Because requirements are grounded in disciplines, they will vary. Requirements should clearly state the behavioral expectations and student responsibilities.

Figure 1-3: *Example of student requirements*

Requirements of the I-Search Paper

1. Relevance: Choose a topic that addresses an issue related to the umbrella focus of "Tikkun olam" or "Repair the world."

2. Passion: Choose a topic that you know little about and one about which you are passionately interested in learning more. This may very well be the most important decision you make during this unit.

3. Organization: There are 5 sections to the paper and multiple steps in completing each section. Complete all steps within each section. I will guide you through the steps of the project and give you due dates. If you are organizationally challenged, do not panic; I will help you. Learn to advocate for yourself, and let me know when you need assistance.

4. Writing Process: All sections of the I-Search paper require a minimum of 3 drafts, 1 self-edit, and a minimum of 1 peer-edit. The focus of the self- and peer-edits are outlined on the self- and peer-edit sheets and focus largely on content and structure. Editing is serious business and requires targeted and explicit feedback. To be effective, be specific in your suggestions and record them in the comment column of the edit sheet.

5. Polished Drafts: While grammatical errors should be corrected throughout the editing processes, one final edit for conventions alone should be made before declaring that your paper is in final draft form.

6. Form—1st Person: Write the first three sections in 1st person—use the pronoun "I".

7. Form—3rd Person: Write the final section, What I Learned in 3rd person—do not use the pronoun "I".

8. Sources: Use a minimum of 6 sources; one must be an interview with a person who has some expertise in your topic.

9. Citations: Use easybib.com to manage your citations; establish an account and provide me with your ID and password.

10. Accountability: You will have some class time to work on your paper, but much of the work will be done at home. Because peer-editing and interviewing involve working with others, think about their time and plan accordingly. Expect to be working on this paper at home every night.

B. Identify due dates. Use a blank calendar and post-it notes to plan out the unit. Begin by identifying the due dates for each assignment. Using post-it notes allows for easily shifting due dates and lessons to accommodate student needs, time restraints, or school demands.

C. Identify specific instructional lessons. The objectives, rationale, and requirements determine the specific instructional lessons students will need to be successful. For example, if the choice of the topic is completely integral to the project, then you might teach a lesson about searching for suitable topics that ignite passion. If students use Easybib.com to manage their citations, they will need a lesson about using the website. If you have students switch writing from 1st to 3rd person, a brief mini-lesson reviewing the difference might be necessary. Because my students conduct an interview during their research journey, we spend one class on the topic of the fine art of interviewing. In addition to instruction of specific content-based objectives and standards, students will need specific lessons based on the unique aspects of the unit itself. Add to the calendar post-it notes identifying what lessons need to be taught and when.

Figure 1-4: *Examples of instructional lessons to support I-Search process*

Mini-Lessons for the I-Search Paper

1. Introduction to the I-Search Paper—Introduction and description
2. The Seven Domains of Lifelong Learning in the I-Search
3. Pacing Guide and Requirements
4. Choosing a Researchable Topic
5. Introduction to What I Know—requirements, models, self/peer-edit sheets, rubric
6. Introduction to What I Want to Know—Developing your guiding question, requirements, notes, models, self/peer-edit sheets, rubric
7. Introduction to Research Journey—requirements, models, self/peer-edit sheets, rubric
8. MLA Citation—Vetting sources, using Easybib.com (Introduction to website, establishing an account, building a Works Cited page)
9. Summarizing and Note Taking from sources
10. The Art of Interviewing
11. Introduction to What I Learned—requirements (shifting to 3rd person), models, self/peer-edit sheets, rubric
12. In-text Citations—academic transitions

D. Map lessons on calendar. After identifying the specific lessons to teach directly, I put them on post-it notes and add them where they fit logically on the calendar. In my school district, instruction in literacy is delivered in a workshop model that balances instruction with practice. This unit requires some class time for instruction and some class time for researching and writing. It is important, therefore, to let students know which days they will be given class time to research and write and which days will be instructional so that they can pace themselves through the unit effectively. Because I normally begin this unit of study in the middle of October, I do not have to set class time aside to instruct my students in how to effectively self- and peer-edit, as they have already learned this process. It is important to note that this unit of study requires students to work every night at home in order to remain on target with regard to due dates.

E. I-Search and the Common Core State Standards. I teach reading and writing (English Language Arts), and within this unit alone, I address the CCSS in 4 out of the 5 areas: Reading Standards for Informational Text, Writing Standards for all three writing genres (narrative, argument, and informative/explanatory) as well as research, Speaking and Listening, and Language. As a capstone to the unit, I have my students present their findings to their class and in so doing cover more of the CCSS for Speaking and Listening, specifically in the areas of presentation and technology. My district adheres to standards-based reporting for assessment, and the rubrics and edit sheets discussed in the following chapter break down the Anchor Standards in more detail. Appendix 1–3 lists the 8th grade CCSS addressed by this unit of study broken down by the various sections of the I-Search paper.

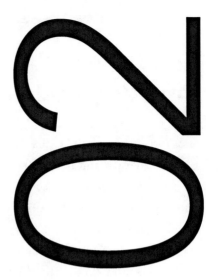

What I Know/
What I Want to Know

When you reach the end of your rope, tie a knot in it and hang on.
—American Proverb

Effective researchers and critical thinkers in general, take an inquiry stance. They examine the beliefs and assumptions they harbor about a topic and identify what it is they would like to or need to learn about that topic. They figure out what they don't know. When making an honest inquiry, the researcher may discover that what he or she thought or believed is, in fact, not true. Questions may lead to more questions or unexpected or unwanted answers. Taking an inquiry stance requires courage. It is, therefore, critical that the environment in which the I-Search occurs is safe for students and teachers to take risks, to admit to not knowing, and to commit to finding answers, no matter what they are. The lessons that follow address how to foster a safe community that celebrates an inquiry stance as students move through the What I Know and the What I Want to Know sections of the I-Search paper.

LESSON 1:
Introducing I-Search

First impressions are critical in shaping our ideas and attitudes towards an issue or a person, and for introducing I-Search, simulations meet these criteria because they appeal to all learning styles and draw on a multitude of skills. If designed correctly, the simulation will immerse students in learning critical content while giving them an emotional understanding of the significance of that new knowledge. As a result, the intellectual and emotional lessons learned will serve as the "knot at the end of the rope" when the individual is faced with challenges later on during the project. If time permits, I strongly suggest introducing the I-Search unit with a simulation designed to illustrate the value of research in everyday life and to expose the multitude of variables that researchers must consider for their work to be successful.

Step 1. Simulation for Introducing I-Search

In designing this simulation I exploited young adolescents' rush to grow up by choosing a focus that would emotionally appeal to my students—buying their first car. Here is the procedure:

1. Ask students to pretend that they are about to purchase their first car. What car would that be? Do they have a "dream car?" For homework the night before I-Search introduction, ask students to: identify that car by make and model; provide basic information often considered when buying a car such as cost and miles per gallon. Encourage them to bring in pictures; to select the color, trim, and accessories they would like; and to be prepared to share their chosen cars with the class the following day.

2. The next day, divide the class into groups of 4 or 5 and ask them to share their "first cars" with one another. Each group could vote on their favorite car to share with the whole class.

3. Once students have shared their chosen cars, distribute to each group a profile of a specific customer who needs to purchase a car. For example, one group receives a profile of an 18-year-old student who works part-time and attends community college; another group receives a profile of a college junior who needs a car to commute to an internship and whose parents have provided him or her with an allowance. Another

profile is that of a 22-year-old who is beginning their first job. Each group then must identify a vehicle that will meet—both financially and physically—the criteria found in the profile. Often, students overlook the hidden costs of owning a vehicle such as the cost of maintenance, fuel, and insurance. Sending groups back to the drawing board to incorporate these elements provides a valuable lesson in research— sometimes you have to revisit your choices.

4. After each group has completed their findings, they report out to the rest of the class to demonstrate the power of the collective mind, placing students into the role of teacher. At the end of the simulation, facilitate a class discussion of the lessons learned as the students reflect on the process and their own experience.

Step 2. Description of process.

Review the handout, "I-Search Description" (Figure 2-1), and answer questions students raise about the paper and the process. Display the document for the class and model the process of annotating by identifying the important information in each paragraph and making notes in the margins. Encourage students to follow your lead using their hard copies.

Figure 2-1: *Description of I-Search*

The I-Search Paper

1. I-Search papers are based on the idea that good research comes from a desire to learn something. So, choose a topic about which you are anxious to learn more.

2. The I-Search paper is written in first-person because your opinion and judgment of the information you discover is an important part of the process and the paper.

3. The information you already know about the topic of your research is important, and you will include it in your paper.

4. All research, even buying a car, begins with a question. You will identify the questions for your research, keeping flexible enough to know that as you gain more knowledge, you may develop more questions or refine your old ones.

5. In real life, many times you begin to learn about new things through conversations. Conversations with people who know something about your topic are important for your I-Search paper. One of the required sources is an interview with an expert on your topic.

6. Experts write books, articles, and websites, and you need to know what the experts who spend much of their time learning about your topic have to say about that topic.

7. When you come to the end of your search, you will share through your paper what you have learned.

8. You will record in a bibliography all the sources of information used in your search.

The Format of Your Paper will be:

1. **What I Know**—Write one or two paragraphs covering what you already know about your topic. Include not only what background you have in this topic, but any experiences you have had and tell where and how you came to know this information. Share why you are curious about learning more about this topic. *The information here does not need to be accurate.* In fact, we can learn a great deal from the assumptions we hold that we later discover are not grounded in truth. So, remember it is important you be honest here, not necessarily correct.

2. **What I Want to Know**—Write one or two paragraphs in which you present the questions you desperately want to answer through your research about your topic. Although you will have a number of questions about your chosen topic, there will be **one main guiding research question** that will need my approval before you begin your research. This is the most critical piece of any research as the questions you write will frame and guide your search. They will direct you to your sources and keep you focused throughout the process. This process will take more time than you think, so make sure you allot the time to do it well.

3. **Research Journey/Source Notes**—Write separate summaries of three out of your required minimum of six sources. You will begin by putting the source into a format called "work cited." The first paragraph will describe for the reader how you found and vetted the source. After carefully reading the source, you will then summarize for the reader the pertinent information from that source, taking care to connect that information to the questions you have identified in

the What I Want to Know section. Also include in this section questions that arise because of any new information you may have discovered in the source. After summarizing the information, conclude by sharing your opinion of the perspective/s and information presented in the source. Include at least one interview/conversation, one article or book, and one website, for a total of three different stories.

4. **What I Learned**—In this section, you reflect on all the research you did and explain what you have learned, the questions you have answered as well as new questions that your research raised. This section will shift to a more formal writing format. It will include an introduction in which you share the thesis (often the guiding question rephrased into a statement) that directed your research. You will then write several paragraphs in which you share with your reader not only what you learned, but also how that new knowledge has changed your thinking about the topic. You will need to support your new learning with evidence pulled from your sources and cite those sources in your text. You will finish this section with a powerful conclusion that clearly summarizes your newfound knowledge, emphasizing its importance.

5. **Reflection**—In this final paragraph you describe your thoughts about your journey and demonstrate how you have grown as a learner and a researcher through this process.

6. **Works Cited**—Here's where you list the sources you've used for your paper according to specific guidelines (MLA). List all sources from your Research Journey and any other sources that you cited in your paper. You need a minimum of six on the list.

Step 3. List questions.

As homework, move the students into the first step of the I-Search, finding a topic of interest. Ask students to watch the world news (not the local—it tends to be less substantive) on TV or online, and to identify issues raised during the broadcast that pique their interest. Students then list questions they have about each issue they identified and prepare to share in class the following day. In addition to the broadcast issues, students list other topics of interest to them plus questions they have about those issues.

LESSON 2:
Settling on a topic: *What I Know*

One of the most critical steps to the I-Search paper is identifying a topic in which there is an enduring interest—no easy task. I often tell my students that choosing a topic to research is as significant as choosing their next boyfriend or girlfriend, as the time spent with this topic will most likely be longer than that spent with their last boyfriend or girlfriend. This makes them laugh, but also drives home the point. If you're going to spend six weeks with something, you darn well better love it! Appendix 2-1, "Finding a Researchable Topic," will help you guide students through the process.

Step 1. Building prior knowledge.

Students gain support to finding topics of high-interest to them through many strategies: field trips (real or virtual), videos, homework, debates, discussions, selected readings, etc. I have a multi-faceted approach to providing background knowledge in support of students selecting their topics. Because my theme is "Tikkun Olam" ("Repair the World"), I assign the homework of watching the world news, which introduces students to a variety of problems of which they may be unaware. Also, my daily read alouds give me a forum to introduce a variety of issues over the weeks preceding the I-Search paper. When I pull the read aloud stories from current newspapers, students can often gain background knowledge to help them understand issues later addressed in the newscast. I have also shown short videos introducing particular issues such as *The Girl Effect* or the *Universal Declaration of Human Rights*, which serve to introduce students to real-world issues and current solutions tied to my overarching theme. As a result, when my students walk into class, their list of topics garnered from the newscast and read alouds is fairly substantial.

Step 2. Share the lists.

Ask students to turn to a peer and share their lists. Their instructions include being good listeners and asking questions or sharing their own knowledge on a topic of interest. This is an introduction to skills that will be addressed more thoroughly during the interview part of the research process.

Step 3. Compile class master list.

After all the lists are shared, as a class we begin to compile a master list. Students list topics randomly on the board and then sort those topics into categories such as issues related to the environment, animal rights, politics, human-rights, gender bias, etc. This has the added benefit of introducing students to the process of categorizing information by ideas, a skill they will later draw from when writing the What I Learned section of the I-Search paper.

Another equally effective approach, though one that requires more time, is to have the students brainstorm a list of questions as opposed to topics. This strategy allows for the exploration of an issue, modeling the metacognitive process needed to uncover the real issue and its importance. For example, a question posed by a student such as, "What's up with the Easter Bunny?" might at first glance, seem frivolous (and, in the 8th grade, probably was intended so). However, given the opportunity to follow a line of questioning, an important issue may be uncovered. Through a series of questions, the topic of heathen ideology and its role in current religious practices can be uncovered. From there, it isn't a far leap to a number of issues such as the role of religion in politics or the argument for or against the separation of church and state. Who knew the Easter Bunny could be so controversial?

Step 4. Discuss topics with parents.

Once students have discussed a variety of topics, they discuss their ideas with their parents. Involving parents is critical for several reasons: (1) they often have a passion for an issue that can help ignite a passion within their child, and (2) because of the controversial nature of some of the topics students choose, parental permission is essential. The goal of the parent-student discussion is for the student to identify 5 issues in which he or she can sustain interest throughout the project—and which the parent(s) will approve. Students and parents sign a letter stating all are in agreement of the 5 topics selected. Appendix 2-2 is a sample of the parent letter including the topic list and signoff.

LESSON 3:
Setting the Pace and Scheduling

For those young adolescents struggling with organization and follow-through, this unit provides opportunities to strengthen their Strategic Awareness skills. To help students be successful in meeting multiple requirements, steps, and due dates, I model strategies for remembering them.

Although I do provide handouts outlining all of these and I post the information on my website, experience shows that if I distribute and then review them in class, students do not retain the detail necessary to work successfully. Therefore, I take the opportunity to teach students the fine art of note taking, modeling the Cornell notes format as I explain each requirement prior to them receiving any requirements in writing.

Step 1. Review the requirements/model Cornell note taking.

Have students transfer the information for each I-Search section from the I-Search Description handout to their Cornell note sheet. Writing the requirements for each section in their own words reinforces the information they have already seen and heard. Appendix 2-3 includes instructions for and a sample model of Cornell notes.

Step 2. Introduce pacing.

Introduce the information in the handout "Pacing Yourself Through the Project" (Appendix 2-4) as students take notes. My goal is to help my students create a schedule that will keep them on track for submitting their work not only on time, but also with the highest possible quality. Therefore, I begin by establishing the eight steps to the writing process that my students are required to follow. Those steps begin with an initial draft, include both a self- and peer-edit, and end with a fourth, polished draft for each section of the paper. If time is an issue, it is here where some time may be saved. By requiring fewer drafts, each section will require less time, though the quality of the final draft may suffer. I then review each section of the I-Search paper, reviewing the requirements (again) and providing the estimated time required needed to complete each section. They record due dates in their notes.

Step 3. Scheduling the process.

Once students take these notes, they record all due dates for each section in the calendars of their assignment notebooks. After recording all the due dates, students identify in their notes the number of days each section should take to complete and, on their calendar, count backwards to identify the day they should begin writing their first draft. My intent is to teach my students how to pace themselves through a long project by walking them through the process: identifying the requirements of the task, determining the time necessary to meet those requirements, and scheduling the work on a personal calendar in order to meet the deadlines. At this age, they are not always cognoscente of the time required to complete a task and, as a result, they rush to complete assignments, often sacrificing quality and depth of thought in the process. This exercise slows them down and illustrates the value of mapping out a plan of action. See Appendix 2-5 for an example of a schedule for an I-Search project.

Step 4. Format requirements.

Once the calendar is established, students finalize the note taking by recording the formatting requirements for the paper. Not until students have taken the notes and recorded the due dates in personal calendars do I distribute "Pacing Yourself Through the Project," "Scheduling the Process," and the format requirements (Appendix 2-6: Student Checklist). By the end of this lesson, the students have several resources with answers to questions that may arise during the unit.

LESSON 4:
Writing *What I Know*

In this section begins the actual writing—and students are writing about what they don't know! One of the most difficult tasks I face during the I-Search paper unit is convincing my students that it is acceptable to not know much about their chosen topic: in fact, it is preferred. Even more difficult is convincing them that what they state as fact in the What I Know section may actually be false, and *that is also okay*. This is so contrary to their experience in school—celebrating the lack of knowledge rather than being penalized for it—that it may take some time to move students from being paralyzed by fear of making a mistake to actually writing.

Step 1. Support "not knowing."

I find it helpful to begin with a conversation about the beauty of not knowing, because only from there can you go on to experience the thrill of learning.

Step 2. Review requirements, rubric, and edit sheets.

The What I Know section is a short piece, usually consisting of 2 to 3 paragraphs in which the students share what they know about their topic, describe the experiences they have had with the topic, and tell what exactly piqued their curiosity about their chosen issue.

This is narrative writing and adheres to the Common Core Standards outlined for that genre of writing. In addition, other CCSS addressed are those related to writing with relationship to development, organization, and style and the editing process. Class discussions and mini-lessons center around addressing these standards and the skills and ideals embedded within them. In my district, we use standards-based reporting to assess students. As a result, the What I Know standards-based rubric (Appendix 2-7) and the What I Know Self-Edit (Appendix 2-8) and What I Know Peer-Edit sheets (Appendix 2-9) pull directly from the CCSS being addressed. The student-friendly language of each standard in the rubric helps students identify exactly what they should strive to accomplish. The self- and peer-edit sheets focus on content as well as elements of good writing. Before introducing any assignment, I review and make available the rubric and any self- and peer-edit sheets so that my students are aware of the target they are trying to hit. Content area teachers would need to address the standards tied to their discipline and the objectives of the particular unit of study they are addressing. Whatever assessment tool is used, it is important for students to have in writing the desired outcomes available from the beginning. Taking the time to critically analyze those outcomes and what is needed to meet them will not only increase student success, but also provides an opportunity to model and instruct critical reading skills. After reviewing the requirements, rubric, and edit sheets, I share models of What I Know sections written by former students such as those in Figure 2-2. We discuss the strengths of each and what, if anything, might strengthen those pieces. Once all questions are addressed, students begin the writing process for the What I Know.

Figure 2-2: *Student examples of* What I Know

What I Know about Poverty in America
By Carl Nelson

I know that poverty in America affects many people differently. One of the effects of poverty can be obesity because if a person doesn't have enough money for a nutritious meal the only other option is fast food because it's cheap. Another effect of poverty is homelessness because if you don't have enough money to pay the bills, your house could be foreclosed.

Some of the ways I came to know this are through reading newspapers, the media, and the news on television, and my own observations. Every day there are stories of people being affected by the economy. They may lose their house or need food stamps for the basic food items. My personal experiences with poverty are seeing homeless people on the streets, begging for any spare change, or knowing someone that works more than one job to get a little extra money.

I'm interested in poverty in America because it is such a big problem in our society. Also because poverty is leaving a huge impact on many Americans and leaving them helpless without houses, food and no one to support them.

The Culture of Beauty
By Maddie Howard

What I Know

I first came upon the topic The Culture of Beauty while watching an episode of one of my family's favorite television series, *Glee*. This is a show about a dysfunctional group of teens who come together and form a school Glee club, despite the fact that it was thought to be un-cool by many. There was one particular scene that happened to catch my eye. One of the lead female roles, Rachel, was contemplating whether or not to have plastic surgery on her nose so it could be refined and corrected. As a child, Rachel thought her nose to be something unique, most definitely not what her classmates would perceive as unattractive. She thought more seriously about a nose job when she reached high school, where her peers began to tease her about her somewhat asymmetrical nose. Eventually, she began to believe their taunts and saw herself as ugly. It wasn't until Finn, a friend, confessed to her saying that he found Rachel's nose to be a very defining trait of her appearance, certainly not something to indicate ugliness. It wasn't until this reassurance from Finn that Rachel decided not to go through with the surgery.

I know that I often feel exactly like Rachel did. Sometimes I will stand in front of the mirror and think; *I am so ugly*, wishing with all my might that I will someday be as gorgeous as the girls around me and the girls I see on television. It can be so hard to feel pretty when all that you watch on television is stick thin models strutting around, stunning wardrobe, flawless skin, boys falling for them left and right. When I see these commercials I feel like I can never be as perfect as them. As if I will always be too fat, too much acne, wear the wrong clothes, say the wrong things.

This episode of Glee had a big impact on my idea of beauty. I began to realize that beauty could be defined in a number of ways, because each man or woman has different tastes on the kind of person that appeals to them. In my opinion, beauty isn't about having the perfect figure or the all-American face, otherwise known as perfectly strait blonde hair, blue eyes, and tan skin. Beauty is taking your strong features and knowing how to enhance them in your own ways. Knowing this urged me to want to find out more about what is thought to be attractive and what that causes girls to think about themselves.

I passionately feel that the culture of beauty has an enormous effect on girls of America today. Every day, girls stare at themselves in the mirror and scrutinize about their looks. Girls shouldn't have to feel the need to do this. A majority of teenage girls, including myself, can connect with Rachel's story on an emotional level, because they experienced the same issue of doubting the fact that they are beautiful, regardless of whether others might find them to be.

LESSON 5:
Discovering *What I Want to Know*

The next stage of the I-Search paper is a critical one, as students discover the essential role that questions play in the learning process. At this point students begin to narrow or broaden their focus and develop an effective guiding question that will serve to direct the research and establish the thesis that will be needed in the What I Learned section. I cannot emphasize enough the value of taking time at this stage of the process, as so much depends on this being done well. It is also important to be aware that at this point in the process, the depth of interest a student holds for a topic is uncovered. There are students who, when asked to identify what it is about the topic that holds their interest, are hard-pressed to come up with an answer. When this happens, I will work with a student to uncover a topic that holds more interest. Distributing Appendices 2-11(What I Want to Know rubric) and Appendices 2-12 and 2-13 (self- and peer-edit sheets) will guide students in keeping focused. Appendix 2-14, "Developing a Research Question," will help you guide students through the process.

Step 1. Free write.

Begin by following Ken Macrorie's suggestion to have students free write about their topic. Free writing asks students to write truthfully and very quickly for 10 or 15 minutes about a specific topic, free from any concerns about spelling, grammar, or other constraints placed on more formal writing. By removing from the final product the critical eye of others, as well as their own, free writing encourages the writer to get to the truth of something (Macrorie, 1988). It encourages free association and helps students uncover what exactly draws them to the topic they have chosen.

Step 2. Consider audience and purpose.

Guide them toward developing an inquirer's stance by asking them to consider their audience and their purpose. Ask students to free write responses to questions such as, "Why will my readers care about this issue?" "What might they already know about the topic?" and "What might they need to learn?" The answers to these questions will help to uncover their intended purpose and define the primary role they will adopt throughout the project. For example, a student's interest and focus may dictate that they take on the role of

- **Advocate,** an individual who speaks for those who cannot speak for themselves; promotes a specific point of view and often includes a call to action.

- **Educator**, a presenter of information for the purpose of informing the reader about a specific topic; may direct the reader to additional sources for more information.

- **Reporter** presents with the sole purpose of informing the reader, with bias kept to a minimum; provides supporting evidence for multiple sides of an issue.

Roles are not exclusive. These roles may not necessarily be exclusive, but it is important for them to recognize when they are assuming a specific role on their issue. Certainly, all research is intended to educate the reader, and so the role of educator will play a significant role in this project. Given that the Research Journey is a summary of the information within a source, my students will find themselves assuming the role of reporter at times. A colleague of mine asks her students to design and implement a plan addressing their topic and resulting in some action to "repair the world" which requires them to take on the role of advocate.

Value of knowing the roles. By acknowledging that they are advocating a particular stand on an issue, they begin to recognize their own bias that then allows them to effectively refute or qualify opposing claims or alternative points of view. The role of reporter, which requires that supporting evidence be presented from multiple perspectives held by different stakeholders, forces students to keep an open mind to the various arguments surrounding their topic. I do not hold students to the role they identify at this stage of the process, as the garnering of new knowledge often changes their position on the topic and shifts their purpose. I do, however, find it invaluable to have them consider these possible roles and how they impact their writing as they move through the process.

Step 3. Draft guiding question.

Students list as many potential research questions as they can identify about their topic and, from that list, draft the overall guiding question. To get the ball rolling, I suggest they begin by using the words *who, what, where, when, why,* and *how.* They might also consider the words *should, would,* or *could.* Requiring a minimum of 10 questions forces students to think more deeply about what it is they want to learn about their topic. This exercise illuminates the breadth and depth of their interest in a topic. Very often, students will list 10 questions, but 2 to 4 of those questions ask the same thing. Help students recognize the repetitions and guide them toward expanding their inquiry. If, after some guidance, they are still unable to identify additional questions about their topic, they may have a lack of real interest. On the rare occasion that this occurs, I help the student identify an alternative topic. In contrast, other students may have long, diverse lists of questions requiring additional work to narrow those topics into manageable pieces. Talking with these students about their interest often helps identify their main focus.

MINI-LESSON:

How to analyze questions to narrow or broaden the topic

Step 1. Model process.

Select one student's list of questions and model the metacognitive process needed to determine the guiding question that will frame and direct that student's research. For example, one of my students, Kyle, who was interested in the topic of global warming, listed the following questions:

1. Why do people deny global warming?

2. When did it start?

3. How fast of a pace is the world warming?

4. Is it just natural?

5. What factors contribute to global warming?

6. What is being done about it?

7. Could there be a permanent solution?

8. What prevents people from believing in global warming?

9. What are some of the impacts of global warming?

10. What role does politics play in it?

Kyle then drafted his potential guiding question: *What role does politics play in global warming and what is its stand in it?* Displaying Kyle's work as a model, I walked the class through the process of determining the primary focus and authoring the guiding question. Kyle's questions reveal that he has a perspective about global warming. He believes it is occurring, and he is knowledgeable enough about the topic to know there is some debate about its authenticity. The first thing I did was encourage students to discern the bias presented by the kinds of questions he asked and the language he used to ask them. I tell my students that it is impossible not to have an opinion on a topic about which they are passionate, but it is essential that they recognize that bias so that during the act of research they seek out alternative perspectives to challenge their thinking. I then sort the questions into categories such as cause, effect, social, economic, or, as in this case, political themes.

Kyle's guiding question shows that his interest rests largely in the political aspects of the issue and what might cause the debate. Questions 2–5 and 9 from his list are inquiries designed to define and understand the actual process of global warming. The role people play in the issue and, more specifically, politics, is the focus of questions 1, 6–8, and 10 and is prominent in his draft of his guiding question. After a short conversation in which Kyle talked about his interest in the topic, we rewrote his guiding question to state, *What are the political and economic issues in the global warming debate?* Our discussion led to the role of money in the acceptance or denial of the existence of the phenomena. Using the category of economics was a way to focus the research to include this aspect.

Step 2. Teacher approval of guiding question.

I approve all guiding questions prior to students' writing the *What I Want to Know* section. The guiding question is critical to the process, as it serves to guide the research and provides the framework for the thesis that will be used in the final section of the paper.

Step 3. Turning questions into statements.

Experience has taught me students' biggest challenge to writing the *What I Want to Know* is writing it in such a way that it does not result in a simple list of questions. As a literacy teacher, I do a mini-lesson that demonstrates how to turn questions into statements to create a rhythm to students' writing that keeps the reader engaged.

As Figure 2.3 shows, in Kyle's What I Want to Know section, he avoided just listing his questions by describing his curiosity about the topic.

If teaching fluency in writing is not a major concern in your content area, the What I Want to Know section might be a list that includes a well-written guiding question and other, smaller questions, saving time in both the writing and the assessing of this section.

Figure 2-3: *Student example of* What I Want to Know

What I Want to Know
By Kyle Keane

For this research paper, I am interested in learning about global warming. I wanted to research this topic after watching a movie called *An Inconvenient Truth,* and after studying our political advertisement unit in our literacy class this year. Although these two events took place some years apart from each other, I formulated many questions. My main question is: What are the political and economic issues pertaining to the debate about global warming?

In order to answer this, I need to gain background knowledge on this topic of interest. However, I have to answer smaller questions guiding my research. One of these questions is why do people deny the facts of global warming? I hear this on the news all the time; people either saying things to credit or discredit the evidence presented. I do not know who to believe now. Likewise, I wish to know if this well-known issue is naturally occurring or a problem created by humans.

Furthermore, after seeing all the places that this problem occurs in the world, I wonder what role politics play in the debate of global warming. Moreover, there are all these arguments taking place. Some people argue that the rising temperatures and sea levels are the result of human pollution, while others claim it's the world's natural cycle and the earth is the cause of all this commotion. It's puzzling to me which side is right or wrong.

This issue creates qualms in my head, dragging me first to one side of the issue then to the other, and I do not know what is true or what is not. That is why I came up with my main question that will guide me through all of my research, and that question is: What are the political and economic issues in the global warming debate? I hope that I will find all the correct answers to these questions so my hunger for answers will be satisfied.

Great quote

Research Journey

If we knew what it was we were doing, it would not be called research, would it?
—Albert Einstein

The actual act of research requires individuals to draw on a host of skills essential to life. These skills are addressed throughout the Research Journey. The critical curiosity needed to raise questions serves to pique interest and, as a result, engagement in life. The lessons learned from the Research Journey evolve from this premise as students:

- apply critical analysis to determine the validity of a source.

- identify the main ideas and specific evidence used to support those ideas.

- summarize the findings and conjectures of others regardless of whether they support or refute their own.

- discover the power of citations to direct researchers toward possible answers.

- experience the power of conversations to expand knowledge and understanding.

LESSON 6:
Requirements, Format, and Models

Only after my students have successfully completed the process of taking an inquiry stance do they begin the actual research.

Step 1. Review the requirements.

Using Figure 3-1, review the requirements for writing. Over the years I have adjusted the requirements for the Research Journey section of the I-Search based on the time I have available. Although I require students to consult a minimum of 6 sources for their research, they only need to formally write up three of those sources: one website, one article or book, and the interview. Throughout the research journey, I will confer with each student, offering guidance and suggestions. At the end of the time allotted for research, my students will submit all three written research journeys, indicating which one they would like to be assessed using the rubric. See Appendix 3-1 ("Research Journey Standards-Based Rubric") and Appendices 3-2 and 3-3 (self- and peer-edit sheets).

Figure 3-1: *Writing outline and guide for* Research Journey

Writing Outline for Research Journey

MLA Citation: Bolded, Hanging indent

Example:

Gentile, R. and Gentile, D. "How Violent Video Games Are Exemplary Aggression Teachers." *Science Daily.* 14 Nov. 2007. Web. 7 Nov. 2009.
<http://www.sciencedaily.com/releases/2007/11/071113160359.htm>

Introduction *(This may be more than 1 paragraph)*
Describe the process you went through to find this source (i.e. keywords, librarian, peer, teacher, etc.). Tell how you evaluated the website, including the criteria you used. Include the questions you had that you believed this source would answer. You might speak to the reputation of the organization or person and any bias you know the author has. (You can find this out by reading the *About Us* section on a website or entering the author or organization's name

into a search engine). Be sure to describe your process of evaluating bias in your sources in this section of your research journey.

Body Paragraphs *(This may be several paragraphs)*
This is where you share with the reader the main ideas that were expressed in the source along with the evidence used by the source to validate and support those ideas. This is strictly a reporting or summary of the information that pertains to your research question that is found in the source. _You do not argue or debate this information here_.

Conclusion *(This is usually one or two paragraphs)*
This is where you share with the reader any changes in your thinking. Did this source challenge what you believed? Did it support your belief? Did it raise new questions? Answer old ones? Send you to another source? Wrap it up with a simple statement of how you felt this source aided your research.

Step 2. Share models.

Ask your students whether the following Research Journey meets the requirements as they compare it to the rubric. Another well-written example is included in Appendix 3-4.

Figure 3-2: *Student example of* Research Journey

Research Journey 3: Interview By Arrianne Love
Brennan, Marina. Personal Interview. Glen Ellyn: 29 Nov 2012.

For my final research journey, I conducted an interview with Dr. Marina Brennan. I found her online by looking up "self-esteem specialists in Glen Ellyn," and her website came up. I scrolled through, checking out all of the information they had about her. I found out that she had her Masters and Bachelor of Science degree in psychology. After looking through a list of other specialists, I decided that Dr. Brennan would be the most knowledgeable about the topic because of her degrees.

Through the interview, I asked Dr. Brennan a series of questions all revolving around the beauty industry and self-esteem. I was able to gain much knowledge as to what self-esteem really is, and what is being done to prevent it. I found out that self-esteem is the amount of respect you have for yourself, and the willingness to try new things. Some signs of low self-esteem are distress about not being happy, the fear of trying new things, and the way you act around others.

According to Dr. Brennan, the media has a big impact on teenagers. The industry presents artificial images of what they think you're supposed to look like. With the media shooting out so many different images, they give girls insensible feelings about themselves. Faivre told me that her step daughter worked at a modeling agency in New York as part of an internship, and she said that the models put in very long hours working under the hot lights. They had to wear outfits that other models had already worn, all smelly with sweat. The modeling industry isn't as glamorous as it seems. Her step daughter ended up being asked to become a model for the agency, but after seeing how hard the job was, she gave up all ideas about wanting to become a model.

In order to become part of the modeling industry, you have to go in with very high self-esteem. You'll be put under a lot of pressure, so you have to be sure not to lose yourself under pressure. One of my initial thoughts on the impact of models was that if girls see pictures of them, they'll instantly feel down about themselves and wish it was them. According to Dr. Brennan, I was wrong. Cases of low self-esteem start way before someone is introduced to modeling.

Dr. Brennan believes that the parents have a lot to do with low self-esteem. The more parents need something from their kids can really shape self-esteem. The parents' reaction to something becomes the children's reaction. Although, she can't do anything to prevent low self-esteem, she encourages parents to support their child. They need to have a nice base of support in what they do. The children need to have passions, something that they have no pressure to excel in. The child needs mentors in what they do, other than their parents.

After conducting the interview, I was able to answer many of my questions like what exactly is low self-esteem; what are some signs that show low self-esteem; how does the media impact the self-esteem of teenagers; how do people react; and is there anything being done to prevent it? Being able to actually sit down and talk to Dr. Brennan was very helpful. I was able to have a face to face conversation, and actually understand what she was telling me.

Finding Credible Sources

Locating sources and determining their credibility are the first steps in conducting any research.

Step 1. Locating sources.

Invite your district's instructional technology specialist to provide students with a quick overview of what a search engine is and how it locates sources. While some of this information is proprietary, it is helpful for students to understand the critical link between the formula used by the search engine and the keywords students choose when searching for information. Several keys to effective Internet searching are provided including Booleans such as *and*, *not*, and *or*; specific punctuation or symbols such as quotation marks, a plus sign, or a minus sign; and specific word choices such as the use of the word "automobile" instead of the word "car." Because the search engines are constantly changing and updating the tools available for searching databases and the Internet, it is impossible to identify in this chapter all the key elements available for refining a search. However, many search engines provide helpful hints on refining keywords. For example, Google posts recommendations on how to refine keywords to focus a search. (http://www.google.com/intl/en/insidesearch/tipstricks/basics.html)

Step 2. Teach students to determine the value and credibility of sources.

As schools increase their subscriptions to databases that provide vetted sources for research, they render it unnecessary for students to determine the credibility of sources. However, the skill of determining the value and credibility of information on the Internet is a life skill and one I teach regardless of the access to credible databases. In addition to the reputation of a source, it is necessary for students to be aware of any bias a resource might have. For example, if a student is researching animal rights and has only pulled information from organizations with a mission to protect animals, I will ask the student to search other sources without this mission that can corroborate the information or might refute it in order to achieve a fuller comprehension of the issue. Therefore, I require my students to look at specific markers on a website that will help them determine the credibility and point of view of the source. They are to look for any bias that may be present and are reminded that while bias is not necessarily a negative, it is an important piece in interpreting and understanding the information. Students are required to read the *About Us* section of a site and the mission statement of any organization, if posted. They are encouraged look at the people and foundations that are associated with the organization and conduct additional searches on those individuals if necessary. I provide a Website rubric as guide to help my students ascertain the reliability of a source (see Appendix 3-5).

LESSON 8:
Citations

I address parenthetical citations in the What I Learned section of the I-Search paper. Here, I teach my students to write the citations that will appear on their Works Cited page. Writing citations according to the MLA or APA guidelines can be challenging, especially for websites, so I provide students with a template for the most common sources such as newspapers, books, films, and pamphlets. However, to facilitate the writing of citations, I require my students to set up an account on the website *easybib.com*. Over the years, this website has streamlined their process for constructing citations, so much so, that a student need simply to copy and paste the URL into the software and hit submit. An easy to use app allows students to create a citation by simply scanning the barcode on books. In addition, it keeps a running list of the sources they have accessed, making the creation of their Work Cited page at the end of the unit a painless process (see Appendix 3-6, "Whipping Up Works Cited").

The website also offers a tool labeled "Notes and Outline" that allows students to keep virtual notes from a source and arrange then to form an outline as a first step to writing their research journey. It provides a place for students to save selected evidence from the text and an area to summarize the information found in the text. EasyBib offers a virtual tour that outlines the capabilities of this software feature. The school librarian demonstrates how to use EasyBib when he gives students a walk through the vast array of resources available to them in the library.

LESSON 9:
Conducting an Interview

Perhaps the most valuable source of the Research Journey is the interview with an individual who has expertise in the topic being researched. Teaching students how to request, conduct, and follow up on an interview is critical, as students will be representing you and the school. This lesson focuses on several aspects of the interview process. A student handout, "The Art of Interviewing," Appendix 3-7, gives students information on the phrasing and types of questions, tips on conducting interviews, and note taking sheet/teacher approval form.

Step 1. Finding interviewees.

I send out an email to the staff that identifies all the topics my kids are researching; I ask for those with expertise on the topics whether they would be willing to grant five students an interview. When possible, I try to arrange group interviews to protect staff members' time.

Some of my students research topics like hunger or homelessness. In those cases, local employees of community organizations serving them, such as food pantries, often will grant interviews, sometimes through email (students write up the interview per the requirements rather than just cut and pasting the email).

I monitor closely (send from my email; get parent permission) student email interviews of people in more nationally-based organizations to protect the students. Additionally, many students interview resources they regularly connect to (church, sports, siblings, etc.). I contact personal resources I know with whom I have worked. For example, my students do a service project through an organization that works with refugees and can connect us to interviewees if a student researches a related topic.

If your students have access to Skype, they may be able to interview experts from another part of the world about their topics, or a top-notch expert located beyond the community. Appendix 3-7 includes tips for conducting a successful Skype interview.

Step 2. Purpose.

Have students identify the purpose of their interview. Ask them to consider what type of information can be obtained from an interview that would not necessarily be easily found in another source. It is essential for students to articulate their purpose for requesting an interview, as they will be contacting their interviewee who will need this information to determine if they are capable of answering their questions.

Step 3. Types and phrasing of questions.

Questions are at the heart of any interview, so the types and phrasing of questions are intricate parts of the lesson. Have students phrase their questions so that each is a clear request for limited information related to their purpose. Their word choice should be neutral in tone and show respect for the interviewee. I review the various types of questions and discuss the strength and weaknesses of each. I encourage students to use open-ended primary and secondary questions that allow the interviewee to elaborate and expand on the information being sought. I discourage them from using leading or loaded questions and encourage them to limit closed-ended questions. Role-playing is an effective and entertaining way to teach these lessons, as it effectively demonstrates why leading, loaded, and closed-ended questions are ineffective.

Step 4. Etiquette.

Teach interviewing etiquette, which is also a good topic for role-playing. Ask students to begin the interview by thanking the interviewee for taking the time to be interviewed and insist they send a hand written thank you note afterwards. Role-playing allows for the demonstration of positive body language such as eye contact and an affirmative posture. I prohibit students from attempting to take word-for-word notes and instead counsel them on how to ask permission to record the interview, and, if the answer is no, the proper way to take notes. I also caution them that this in not an "essay test" where a question is asked and an answer is given, but rather a conversation. It is essential that they listen to their interviewee and ask follow-up questions that may not be on their prepared interview sheet. It is often this situation that leads to the best information, and I encourage my students to be comfortable deviating from the script if they find themselves in this situation. Comfort comes with practice, and so multiple opportunities to role-play interviews help achieve this. Finally, students are instructed on the value and importance of using a clearinghouse question such as, "Is there anything else you think I should know about this topic?" as it provides the interviewee the opportunity to share additional information.

Step 5. Plan the interview.

Following the lesson on interviewing, my students complete a plan for their interview that must get my approval. As part of that plan, I ask my students to write the request for an interview that includes why they are contacting the interviewee, where they found his or her name, and if applicable, who referred him or her. The request should include the purpose of the interview and a request for a convenient time during which the interviewee might be available. It might also include times during which my student is available. The plan also requires my students to articulate clearly what they have determined is the purpose of the interview. What do they hope to discover in the interview? They are to follow this with a list of questions they plan to ask. By reviewing this plan with my students, I am able to offer guidance and suggestions to insure a positive experience for all.

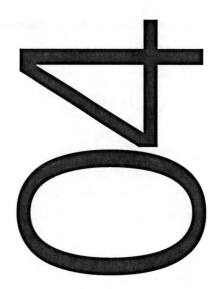

What I Learned

It's what you learn after you know it all that counts.
—John Wooden

At this point in the process, students shift from writing in first person to writing in third person, moving from a more personal style to a formal academic format, though this is not necessary. Staying in the first person provides another opportunity for content area teachers to save some time. For teachers whose focus is on content learned, having students continue to write in first person will reveal the lessons they have learned as a result of their research. Because first person tends to be less intimidating for middle school writers, this can save time.

LESSON 10:
Requirements and Format

I begin by distributing and reviewing "The What I've Learned Guide", Figure 4-1, which includes the criteria, an outline for their research paper, and examples of various parts of the paper. Depending on the time of year in which I assign the I-Search paper, I may need to spend a little time breaking down the elements of a good paper. If I have already taught them how to write an effective introduction and conclusion, then I only review those elements. If, however, I have not, I might need to incorporate that lesson into this unit. Distributing Appendix 4-1 (What I Learned rubric) and Appendices 4-2 and 4-3 (self- and peer-edits) will help students remain focused.

Figure 4-1: What I Learned *Guide*

The *What I've Learned* Guide

The What I Learned section is the actual formal research paper. You will be making a shift in register, from a more personal, casual one in which you use the words 'I' and 'my' to a more formal one, in which you don't. It will involve writing an:

1. *Introduction* that goes from general and narrows down to your thesis (your guiding question rephrased into a statement).

2. *Body Paragraphs* organized, *not by sources* as was done in the Research Journey, but rather, by ideas and concepts discovered in your sources and identified in your thesis.

3. *Conclusion* that revisits your thesis and provides an extension that punches home your 'so what.'

You will need to **support your new learning with evidence pulled from your sources and you need to cite those sources in your text.**

Format:

1. Header: Name, Block #, Date

2. Title: **What I've Learned** bolded and centered

3. Introduction: Begin by introducing your topic and going from general to specific and ending with your thesis. Your thesis is derived from your approved guiding question. That question is changed into a statement.

4. Body Paragraphs 3 - ?: Synthesize all the new knowledge you have learned by focusing on the major findings you uncovered in your search. Structure your paper according to the categories established by your thesis. Each paragraph should address a major idea or concept discovered during your research.

    For example, if your guiding question focuses on factors that led to your topic and what is being done to address the problem, then one of your body paragraphs will begin with a _topic sentence_ that goes something like this: _One of the factors that lead to _____ is (name the factor)._ It is common that each factor would have its own paragraph. After you have discussed all the factors you would then begin a body paragraph with a _topic sentence_ that addresses what is being done to address the problem. It might read something like this: _Fortunately, there are organizations that are trying to help._ You would then discuss all the organizations that are working to solve the issue.

    In each paragraph, share the knowledge you have gained and opinions you have formulated as a result of that new-found knowledge and be sure to support them with examples, stories, or arguments that you found in your sources and that will help the reader understand how you arrived at those conclusions. Be sure to credit the sources from which you have pulled information and distinguish their ideas from your own by citing your sources in your text. You can achieve this by using the academic transitions provided or by following the rules for parenthetical citations outlined by MLA.

5. Conclusion: Conclude your paper with a brief summary of what you have learned and why it is important. Be sure to refer back to your thesis. This is where you emphasize the 'So What' of your paper.

Final Note—Reflection on the Process: After you have completed writing your paper, write a short reflection on the I-Search process. Tell the story of your experience as you moved through this project. Do you feel that you have learned more about your topic than you knew before you started? Did you learn more about the process of researching than you knew before? What challenges did you face? Did you experience any Aha! moments? Do you feel you are more of an expert on your topic now that you have gone through the process? Do you think you learned anything from having gone through this process that will serve you well in high school, college, and life? This reflection should be filled with your personal thoughts and your feelings. You can be honest, just don't be brutal.

Discuss new questions that arose during your research and why those questions were of interest to you. What old knowledge was challenged? How did that make you feel? Feel free to draw conclusions and formulate opinions, but you must support your conclusions with evidence from your sources. Remember it is imperative that you cite the evidence you use. You may also include a personal comment on the I-Search process and any value you see in its ability to help you grow as a learner.

LESSON 11:
Writing a Thesis Statement

Step 1. Write the thesis statement.

Because it is a key component to all writing, so I always walk my students through the process of changing their guiding research question into a thesis statement. While the research journey for some students took them to a different focus than their original guiding question, most students will use their guiding question as a skeleton on which to build their thesis. Tied closely to the thesis is the organization of the paper.

Step 2. Organize by main ideas, not sources.

One of the major difficulties my 8th grade students experience with writing is how to organize their papers when presenting what they have learned. Their first inclination is to organize the paper according to sources by providing a summary of each. I point out to them that they have already done this in their research journeys. The formal What I Learned section is organized differently. Using the thesis as a guide, this section is organized by the main ideas they discovered about their topic or the categories they identified when they authored their guiding questions. For example, my student, Kolin, wrote his guiding question as, *"What are the causes and effects of spinal and head injuries in football, and what is being done to address the issue?"* It makes sense, then, that his thesis became, *"One of the looming problems in football is the concussion. There are several causes and serious effects of the injury, but fortunately, there are steps being taken to address the issue."* He then went on to organize his paper according to the causes, effects, and the steps being taken to minimize this injury in football. To help students sort out the facts, opinions, and changes in their thinking, I use student handout "Summarizing and Synthesizing," Appendix 4-4.

LESSON 12:
Writing *What I Learned*

Some of my students struggle with structuring a paragraph and need some review on the importance of topic sentences or providing evidence along with an explanation of their findings. Depending on the levels within the class, I will address these skills in small groups or on a one-to-one basis.

Step 1. Providing context.

Each year I include a mini-lesson for the entire class on the importance of providing context for the reader. Many of my students feel constrained by their thesis and neglect to include contextual information that facilitates understanding. This problem is particularly associated with writing about a topic about which the author knows a great deal. I remind my students that their reader may not share the same level of expertise on the topic, and so they are responsible for providing enough background information to facilitate their reader's understanding. Adding a contextual paragraph or several sentences within a paragraph that provides enough information to the reader might be necessary and often provides clarity.

Step 2. Using transitions.

Another challenge many of my students face is the use of transitions and how to weave evidence into the body of their paper. I have found that by presenting them with key phrases they can use to weave in their evidence, they are able to improve their writing immensely. Therefore, I take a little time to review the various ways that students can cite their sources and weave in their evidence effectively, adhering to the rules established by MLA or APA guidelines and creating a document that smoothly moves their reader through the new knowledge they have gained.

Example: Introductory phrases such as, *According to Dr. Seuss, . . . or In William Shakespeare's play, Romeo and Juliet, . . .* help students seamlessly incorporate their evidence into their paper. During this lesson, we as a class will brainstorm various ways to introduce sources. For example, one way to avoid sounding redundant when using academic transitions is to focus on verb changes. Dr. Seuss might *state, suggest, argue, or imply.* Changing prepositions achieves the same end. *According* to Shakespeare . . . or In Shakespeare's play . . . These small changes become useful when writing the What I Learned section of the I-Search and present the opportunity to enjoy some word play activities (see Appendix 4-5, "Key Phrases for Citing Evidence"). Figure 4-2 is a student example of What I Learned.

Figure 4-2: *Student example of* What I Learned

What I Learned
By Paige Hardy

What's the most immense hazard to public healthcare? No, it isn't the Affordable Care Act or the severe underfunding of health programs. Antibiotic resistance, or the inability of antibiotics to be able to treat common microbes, has been termed "The greatest threat to public healthcare," by many groups, including the Center for Disease Control and Prevention, or the CDC. Almost every microbe is less susceptible to regular medications (McGowan). After seeing a documentary about this topic, I had many questions relating to biology, economic impact, and causes, but decided to mainly research the history of antibiotic resistance, particularly as it pertains to MRSA, and its prevention.

According to Mrs. Kane, a man named Sir Alexander Fleming accidentally discovered antibiotics. A contaminant got into the Petri dish he was using to grow bacteria, which killed the microbes. Fleming found this interesting, but was unable to isolate the mold. Thirty or so years later two doctors named Howard Florey and Ernst Chain managed to make a medication out of the contaminant named Penicillin. Reportedly, the scientists cautioned that they had found strains that were resistant to the antibiotic during their studies, if they used antimicrobials excessively (Kane). However, the rest of the world was in awe of the drug that had saved the lives of so many soldiers during World War II, and dismissed most cases of antibiotic resistant microorganisms as flukes (Drexler 124).

Garret claims that hospitals had switched to using Methcillin because it was cheaper, so most doctors didn't react to Penicillin resistant strains of a bacterium named Staphylococcus. However, when Methcillin-resistant Staph (MRSA) emerged, well, the doctors were stunned, and attempted to take preventative measures (412). These apparently didn't work, because Staph gained resistance to most antibiotics, like Naficillin and Linezolid, and left only Vancomycin as the drug of last resort (414). Because of the hoard of drug resistance genes MRSA possessed, some health care groups changed its name from Methcillin Resistant *Staphylococcus aureus* to Multidrug- Resistant *Staphylococcus aureus*, although others still keep the original term. Garret persists that even different types of pathogens gained drug resistance, including Streptococcus, Otitis media, known for causing ear infections, Malaria, Tuberculosis, HIV, Salmonella, and E. coli. (414-449) One strain of Streptococcus was resistant to a total of 13 different antibiotics. Another outbreak of a chlorine resistant parasite named Cryptosporidium left 400,000 people sick, earning both the infamous titles of the largest parasitic and waterborne epidemic in the United States of America. This strain was so resistant it could live on Clorox (429-430).

According to Davis, MRSA is relatively common in hospitals, so doctors must know its biology. It's spread by person-to-person contact with a carrier (approximately 1% of the population) or an infected material, usually to people with open wounds. Staph usually starts as a lesion, or abnormal spot, on the skin. If it spreads to the internal organs, then intensive care is necessary. Davis claims that almost 1.2 million people across the globe will die from MRSA this year, due to its mortality rate of 10%. The dangerous diagnosis is confirmed by biopsy, or the examination of cells under a microscope. Vancomycin is the drug of last resort, although some resistant strains to even that have been confirmed.

As the CDC states in their article "Antibiotic Resistance Questions & Answers," they have researched various causes of antimicrobial resistance. According to Todar, germs can go through vertical integration, which is basically a mutation in the gene sequence. There is also horizontal integration, in which the pathogen uses transposins, or special cells, to steal bundles of DNA from other germs. The CDC also claims that if antibiotics don't destroy all of the microbes, the strongest bacteria can survive and reproduce, passing along their genes. This is called partial resistance. The pathogens can change, the CDC mentioned, to destroy, confuse, or neutralize the antimicrobial, rendering it useless ("Antibiotic Resistance Questions & Answers"). Drexler also believes that antibiotic resistance is caused by improper hospital hygiene, and overuse of the drugs originally (134). These drugs extend to antibacterial soap and acne medications ("Antibiotic Resistance Questions & Answers"). Garret adds that low-level antibiotic use in farms is a breeding ground for resistant pathogens, due to partial resistance, noting that it actually created E. coli 0157 (425).

McGowan states that antibiotic resistance has a large economical impact on American society. The CDC estimates 4-5 billion extra dollars are paid each year due to resistance. Almost everybody dealing with the healthcare business is affected. Physicians' pay extra for ineffective antibiotics, healthcare groups must spend money to insure old antibiotics still work, and of course, patients pay for useless drugs, exotic drugs that work, a longer hospital stay, and more costs for tests to determine the drugs their disease is resistant to in the first place.

All of these sources have different ideas for the prevention and containment of resistance. McGowan believes that more funding should be given for research on this topic. Davis wishes for chemically changed Vancomycin that can destroy all current resistant strains to be made available to consumers. According to Mrs. Kane, broad-spectrum antibiotics should be used only as a last resort. On a different note, the

CDC promotes strict following of instructions of both physicians and medication bottles ("Antibiotic Resistance Questions & Answers"). McGowan also lobbies for a better tracking system of disease. However, they all agree that education about the proper usage of antibiotics for both doctors and the general public would help to limit resistance. Stricter hygiene requirements in hospitals could also be beneficial.

In conclusion, I learned many things about the history, causes, biology, economical impact, and prevention of both Staph and antibiotic resistance, answering my questions on these topics. Personally, I believe that education and hygiene in hospitals is the best way to limit resistance. However, I still would like to research the role of MRSA in the food industry, and how penicillin affected World War Two. Now that I know more about the history of antibiotic resistance and its prevention, I will educate others about its past, and what human beings must do to keep these drugs from being obsolete in the future.

Works Cited

Davis, Charles Patrick. "MRSA (Methicillin-Resistant Staphylococcus Aureus) Infections." Medicine Net. Ed. Melissa Conrad Stoppler. Web MD, 1 Sept. 2011. Web. 29 Nov. 2012. <http://www.medicinenet.com/mrsa_infection/article.htm>.

Drexler, Madeline. Emerging Epidemics: The Menace of New Infections. New York: Penguin, 2010. Print.

Garrett, Laurie. "Antibiotic Resistance." The Coming Plague: Newly Emerging Diseases in a World out of Balance. New York: Farrar, Straus and Giroux, 1994. N. pag. Print.

Kane, Annie. "Antibiotic Resistance." Personal interview. 30 Nov. 2012.

McGowan, John E. "Economic Impact of Antimicrobial Resistance." CDC. Center for Disease Control and Prevention, 2 July 2001. Web. 30 Nov. 2012. <http://wwwnc.cdc.gov/eid/article/7/2/70-0286_article.htm#r4>.

Todar, Kenneth. "Bacterial Resistance to Antibiotics." Todar's Online Textbook of Bacteriology. 2008-2012. Web. 30 Nov. 2012 <ttp://textbookofbacteriology.net/resantimicrobial.html>

LESSON 13:
Reflection

Once the students have completed the What I Learned and Works Cited sections, I ask them to reflect on the process and write a short paragraph or two addressing their thoughts and feelings about this unit of study. I want them to consider what they have learned through the process and how it has changed the way in which they learn. I also want them to provide me with feedback about what was valuable in the process, what was confusing or missing, and how I might improve the design of the unit for future students. They are encouraged to share both negative and positive experiences with honesty supported by evidence. Did they experience any aha! moments? Were their aspects of instruction that need clarification or further development? How did the process help them grow? What might I add or delete in order to streamline the process without sacrificing any value?

Time used to reflect on a unit of study is never wasted time. It helps students develop a very important skill required for the development of their Strategic Awareness, one that will serve them well throughout their lifetime. The reflections are also very valuable for me as a teacher in terms of refining and improving my craft. I use the information in these reflections to revise and strengthen the unit of study. Student examples of reflections follow in Figure 4-3.

Figure 4-3: *Student reflections on the I-Search*

Reflection by Nicole Clapp

"Have a great weekend, but start thinking about topics that might interest you, because we'll be researching these topics for at least six weeks while writing the I-Search." When I heard these words come from my literacy teacher, Dr. Bruno, I was really irritated. Having to write a long research paper with 32 drafts was going to be horrible. I thought I'd make the best of it by choosing a really controversial topic that no one else would choose: Teen Pregnancy. I have learned so much from doing this research paper. For me personally, I don't do great with just reading articles and books, as I don't absorb it, so when I wrote each section of the I-Search, it helped me to comprehend the information. I do feel like an expert now. The I-Search paper has allowed me to not only learn the information myself, but also to share it with other people. The writing process is tedious, but I think it will help me leaps and bounds for high school English.

Reflection by Kyle Keane

Looking back upon the I-Search paper, I realize now that I have grown, as a reader, a writer, and a researcher. Before this, I never really thought of myself as a good writer or editor, but after going through all of the specifications needed in each paper, I saw the flaws more easily in both my papers and others, and I saw ways to correct them too. But I did get stressed out on some parts of it too. Cramming this and other homework from all my other class didn't mix well, but it feels good that it's going to finally be over. This has helped dramatically with researching for relevance, and taking good notes. The I-search paper in its whole, no matter how long and stressful is a great time management project, and in addition teaches ways to write in different ways that have previously never been used before.

Reflection by Kolin Kennebeck

During this project, I have learned so much about concussions in football and I have answered all of the questions I had about them. This is important to me because I love the sport of football and want to see it become safer, but still be fun and intense. I play football, so this topic personally affects me, and I don't want to get a concussion. I have also learned so much about the process of researching, and it will help me immensely throughout high school, college, and the rest of my life. It has taught me to check that sources are credible and useful, how to cite sources, how to edit and correct my own papers, and much more. I really liked researching and writing this paper, and I think this assignment should be continued in this class.

Reflection of the Process by Katy Kostolansky

This writing project was a great experience for me. I learned a lot about illegal immigration that I hadn't known before. The research process wasn't different from my past research papers, except for the fact that we were able to access and use a note organizer. This helped me pick out the main ideas and supporting evidence that were in the source I chose. This project involved a ton of work and time to complete each step; however the difference between each section shows how much I really have improved throughout this process. I struggled to find time to complete each part outside of school due to the activities I take part in and the homework I had with other subjects. That would be the only negative thing about the iSearch paper. I was always up late finishing the steps that were due the next day. I felt rushed and due to that I felt like my first draft wasn't written to the level of writing I wish it was. However, when we were allowed class time, I found it beneficial not only to have extra time, but to also be surrounded with people who can help if needed. Overall, I am glad that I had the opportunity to due this project. In general, I feel that the processes we went through will serve me well in high school and throughout life.

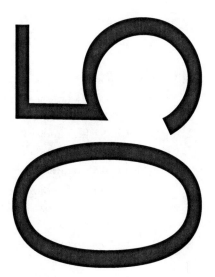

We-Search and Other Time Savers

For the strength of the Pack is the Wolf, and the strength of the Wolf is the Pack.
—Rudyard Kipling

For teachers who are hard-pressed for time and are not primarily teaching the fine art of writing, there are ways to adapt the I-Search process and still meet not only the Common Core Standards, but also the 21st century skills so vital to student success. By grouping students, the I-Search becomes a "We-Search" project. For students, the benefits rest in the development of learning relationships, critical thinking, the expansion of perspective and understandings that come from others, and public speaking skills. For teachers the benefits rest in the instructional time invested during class and the personal time needed to assess. Additionally, it offers the ability to provide real-time feedback and guidance throughout the process.

CCSS addressed. Reading non-fiction text, finding the main ideas, using evidence to support those ideas, and listening and speaking are just a few of the Common Core State Standards addressed by adapting the I-Search to a We-Search. For content area teachers, the CCSS for reading and writing are specific to the discipline and are as follows:

Reading—History/Social Studies

1. **Key Ideas and Details**

   a. CCSS.ELA-Literacy.RH.6-8.1 Cite specific textual evidence to support analysis of primary and secondary sources.

   b. CCSS.ELA-Literacy.RH.6-8.2 Determine the central ideas or information of a primary or secondary source; provide an accurate summary of the source distinct from prior knowledge or opinions.

   c. CCSS.ELA-Literacy.RH.6-8.3 Identify key steps in a text's description of a process related to history/social studies (e.g., how a bill becomes law, how interest rates are raised or lowered).

2. **Craft and Structure**

   a. CCSS.ELA-Literacy.RH.6-8.4 Determine the meaning of words and phrases as they are used in a text, including vocabulary specific to domains related to history/social studies.

   b. CCSS.ELA-Literacy.RH.6-8.5 Describe how a text presents information (e.g., sequentially, comparatively, causally).

   c. CCSS.ELA-Literacy.RH.6-8.6 Identify aspects of a text that reveal an author's point of view or purpose (e.g., loaded language, inclusion or avoidance of particular facts).

3. **Integration of Knowledge and Ideas**

   a. CCSS.ELA-Literacy.RH.6-8.7 Integrate visual information (e.g., in charts, graphs, photographs, videos, or maps) with other information in print and digital texts.

   b. CCSS.ELA-Literacy.RH.6-8.8 Distinguish among fact, opinion, and reasoned judgment in a text.

   c. CCSS.ELA-Literacy.RH.6-8.9 Analyze the relationship between a primary and secondary source on the same topic.

Reading—Science & Technical Subjects

1. **Key Ideas and Details**

   a. CCSS.ELA-Literacy.RST.6-8.1 Cite specific textual evidence to support analysis of science and technical texts.

   b. CCSS.ELA-Literacy.RST.6-8.2 Determine the central ideas or conclusions of a text; provide an accurate summary of the text distinct from prior knowledge or opinions.

   c. CCSS.ELA-Literacy.RST.6-8.3 Follow precisely a multistep procedure when carrying out experiments, taking measurements, or performing technical tasks.

2. **Craft and Structure**

   a. CCSS.ELA-Literacy.RST.6-8.4 Determine the meaning of symbols, key terms, and other domain-specific words and phrases as they are used in a specific scientific or technical context relevant to grades 6–8 texts and topics.

   b. CCSS.ELA-Literacy.RST.6-8.5 Analyze the structure an author uses to organize a text, including how the major sections contribute to the whole and to an understanding of the topic.

   c. CCSS.ELA-Literacy.RST.6-8.6 Analyze the author's purpose in providing an explanation, describing a procedure, or discussing an experiment in a text.

3. **Integration of Knowledge and Ideas**

   a. CCSS.ELA-Literacy.RST.6-8.7 Integrate quantitative or technical information expressed in words in a text with a version of that information expressed visually (e.g., in a flowchart, diagram, model, graph, or table).

   b. CCSS.ELA-Literacy.RST.6-8.8 Distinguish among facts, reasoned judgment based on research findings, and speculation in a text.

   c. CCSS.ELA-Literacy.RST.6-8.9 Compare and contrast the information gained from experiments, simulations, video, or multimedia sources with that gained from reading a text on the same topic.

Writing—History/Social Studies; Science & Technical Subjects

1. Text Types and Purposes

    a. CCSS.ELA-Literacy.WHST.6-8.1 Write arguments focused on discipline-specific content.

    b. CCSS.ELA-Literacy.WHST.6-8.1a Introduce claim(s) about a topic or issue, acknowledge and distinguish the claim(s) from alternate or opposing claims, and organize the reasons and evidence logically.

    c. CCSS.ELA-Literacy.WHST.6-8.1b Support claim(s) with logical reasoning and relevant, accurate data and evidence that demonstrate an understanding of the topic or text, using credible sources.

    d. CCSS.ELA-Literacy.WHST.6-8.1c Use words, phrases, and clauses to create cohesion and clarify the relationships among claim(s), counterclaims, reasons, and evidence.

    e. CCSS.ELA-Literacy.WHST.6-8.1d Establish and maintain a formal style.

    f. CCSS.ELA-Literacy.WHST.6-8.1e Provide a concluding statement or section that follows from and supports the argument presented.

    g. CCSS.ELA-Literacy.WHST.6-8.2 Write informative/explanatory texts, including the narration of historical events, scientific procedures/ experiments, or technical processes.

    h. CCSS.ELA-Literacy.WHST.6-8.2a Introduce a topic clearly, previewing what is to follow; organize ideas, concepts, and information into broader categories as appropriate to achieving purpose; include formatting (e.g., headings), graphics (e.g., charts, tables), and multimedia when useful to aiding comprehension.

    i. CCSS.ELA-Literacy.WHST.6-8.2b Develop the topic with relevant, well-chosen facts, definitions, concrete details, quotations, or other information and examples.

    j. CCSS.ELA-Literacy.WHST.6-8.2c Use appropriate and varied transitions to create cohesion and clarify the relationships among ideas and concepts.

    k. CCSS.ELA-Literacy.WHST.6-8.2d Use precise language and domain-specific vocabulary to inform about or explain the topic.

    l. CCSS.ELA-Literacy.WHST.6-8.2e Establish and maintain a formal style and objective tone.

    m. CCSS.ELA-Literacy.WHST.6-8.2f Provide a concluding statement or section that follows from and supports the information or explanation presented.

    n. (See note; not applicable as a separate requirement)

2. **Production and Distribution of Writing**

    a. CCSS.ELA-Literacy.WHST.6-8.4 Produce clear and coherent writing in which the development, organization, and style are appropriate to task, purpose, and audience.

    b. CCSS.ELA-Literacy.WHST.6-8.5 With some guidance and support from peers and adults, develop and strengthen writing as needed by planning, revising, editing, rewriting, or trying a new approach, focusing on how well purpose and audience have been addressed.

    c. CCSS.ELA-Literacy.WHST.6-8.6 Use technology, including the Internet, to produce and publish writing and present the relationships between information and ideas clearly and efficiently.

3. **Research to Build and Present Knowledge**

    a. CCSS.ELA-Literacy.WHST.6-8.7 Conduct short research projects to answer a question (including a self-generated question), drawing on several sources and generating additional related, focused questions that allow for multiple avenues of exploration.

    b. CCSS.ELA-Literacy.WHST.6-8.8 Gather relevant information from multiple print and digital sources, using search terms effectively; assess the credibility and accuracy of each source; and quote or paraphrase the data and conclusions of others while avoiding plagiarism and following a standard format for citation.

    c. CCSS.ELA-Literacy.WHST.6-8.9 Draw evidence from informational texts to support analysis reflection, and research.

21st century skills addressed. A We-Search paper addresses the same 7 domains of lifelong learning that an I-Search paper addresses. By comparing the collective beliefs gathered during the What I Know sections to the collective knowledge represented in the What I Learned section, students can clearly see growth in learning. The development of questions through discussions pushes students to reach further intellectually as each student within a group shares and builds on their critical curiosity. Sharing the connections they make as they build deeper and broader conceptual understandings leads students to more rigorous and challenging work. A group approach provides a unique opportunity for collective ideas to develop new ways to see things, leading to new ideas and drawing from each student's creativity and learning relationships. Within those learning relationships, students will find the resilience to push through together the challenges and obstacles they will encounter, developing new and more effective strategies along the way.

Converting the I-Search to a We-Search

1. **Topic:** Ask groups of students to identify a current problem related to the general topic of a unit under study. For example, in a science unit on weather, groups of students could research various aspects of contemporary weather events such as the earthquake in Haiti or Hurricane Katrina. In a social studies unit, groups of students could research the wide breadth of historical events that occurred during a specific time and/or place.

2. **What I Know:** Rather than each student writing a What I Know, each group could employ the same critical thinking skills by making a list. After each student makes a list, the group compiles their collective facts and assumptions. The group then, in the process of organizing their pre-knowledge of the topic they have chosen to research, identifies shared beliefs and assumptions as well as those that are in direct conflict with one another. The potential for deep, thoughtful conversations exists when one student believes something to be true while another holds an assumption that stands in opposition to that belief. Exploring the source of one's belief can be very eye-opening and allows students to "see through new eyes." Continuing our weather example, students might have items on their list such as those in Figure 5-1.

Figure 5-1: *We-Search example of* What I Know

What I know: Hurricane Katrina

Shared beliefs and assumptions	Conflicting beliefs and assumptions
The city of New Orleans was devastated.	Areas in the city are still devastated/New Orleans is back to normal.
FEMA is part of the federal governments' response to natural disasters.	The levies have been rebuilt to withstand another Hurricane like Katrina/The levies around New Orleans are still inadequate.
Many people suffer in these kinds of storms.	Katrina is a product of global warming/Katrina is not a product of global warming.

3. **What I Want to Know:** Students can cover the What I Want to Know section through conversation and debate. Rather than writing a formal paper, each group could, through discussion, list every question each member has and then craft a guiding question that all group members will use as their GPS through the research process. In the case of the Katrina example a list of questions might look something like this.

   a. How many people died in the disaster?

   b. How many people became homeless?

   c. How did the government evacuate so many people? Was it hard? Why or why not?

   d. Why would some people decide to stay?

   e. Who helps in a disaster?

   f. What happens to pets?

   g. How much time did they have before they knew the storm would hit New Orleans?

   h. What makes tracking a storm hard?

   i. What happens to sick people in hospital?

   j. What damage does the storm do to a city?

   k. How does a storm become so strong?

   l. Is the power of the storm related to global warming?

   m. What help is available to people?

n. Who helps in disasters?

o. What were people told to do when they knew the storm was coming?

p. Was there anything that could have been done to minimize the damage? If so, why wasn't it done?

From that list of questions, it is obvious that this group of students is curious about the impact a strong storm has on people, the help that is available to them before, during, and after the storm, and how science is able to track and explain powerful storms such as Katrina. From this list a guiding question might read something like, "What was the cause and impact of Hurricane Katrina on the city of New Orleans, and what was the nation's response prior to, during, and after the storm hit?" or "How did the scientific, political, and social, communities respond to Hurricane Katrina? What lessons were learned?"

4. **Research Journeys:** Group members divide the necessary Research Journeys among themselves and then report out the findings to the group. In the case of the Katrina example, the research could be divided by the science behind the storm, the politics behind the decisions to the threat and the aftermath of the storm, and the various non-political organizations that responded to the disaster. Each student in the group would practice the same skills involved in the more traditional Research Journey. Students would identify the big ideas of a source and the evidence used to support those ideas. As they share these with their group, students demonstrate their ability to locate the main ideas and the evidence used to support those ideas within a text, addressing the Common Core Standards for the reading of non-fiction text and allowing them to sharpen their ability to summarize and report out to others. If sources include interviews, 2 to 3 students can conduct them; if groups are larger than that, they can conduct multiple interviews allowing all students to learn and practice the skill of speaking directly to experts in the field. Group research journeys look exactly like individual research journeys.

5. **What I Learned:** Rather than writing a full *What I Learned* paper, each group could present their findings to the class. Well-organized and fluent presentations follow the same requirements of a written paper. A well-written thesis, clear topic sentences, strong evidence, parenthetical citations, precise and concise word choices, and effective transitions exist not only in writing, but also in an effective presentation. Developing a stage presence and the ability to develop public speaking skills is a life skill that will develop self-confidence while it addresses the Common Core Standards in Listening and Speaking. Asking students to use Prezi, PowerPoint (Word)/Keynote (Mac), Google Presentation, Glogster Online Poster offers the opportunity to introduce new technology. (See Appendix 5-1).

6. **Reflection:** The reflection piece serves two purposes: 1) to assist students in building their strategic awareness by having them reflect on the process and their contribution throughout that process by determining what they did that worked well and what might they need to change in their own behavior to improve, and 2) to assist the teacher in fine-tuning and strengthening the unit plan in order to maximize student engagement and learning. This would be the piece of the We-Search paper that I would require be done individually. Students need the ability to write honestly about their experience. If there was some difficulty within the group, students need to be able to share that feedback safely.

7. Presentation Rubric. See Appendix 5-2.

Grouping your students: The grouping of students is an art, and should be done purposefully. Ultimately a teacher makes these decisions after considering a multitude of factors. I rarely allow my students to determine their own groups, as I have found that the dynamics and power structures that exist carry over to group work in the classroom. As a result, those individuals who could take on more leadership roles and those that need to learn to allow others to lead are denied the opportunity to do so. In addition, there is always a student or two who have no friends in the class and are painfully reminded of that when students form their own groups. In the case of a We-Search paper, an interest in the topic is a key-motivating factor, and so groups can be created around this premise. Soliciting a prioritized list of interests from each student prior to publicizing this interest will avoid friends duplicating lists for the sole purpose of being placed in a group together.

Teaching the art of collaboration: The We-Search approach to the I-Search paper requires some instruction in how to work collaboratively in a positive way. Teachers often assume students know how to do this, as they are often happy to do so, but my experience has shown otherwise. As a result, before doing any group work, I establish parameters within which all groups must function as well as requirements to which all group members must adhere.

Nonnegotiable behavior:

1. Actively listen to all ideas.

2. Voice and consider all suggestions BEFORE changing topics.

3. Record all ideas BEFORE any decisions are made.

4. Democratically arrive at your final decisions.

Establish a "Covenant of Behavior":

Each group creates a set of rules that insures they use a democratic process to make decisions.

1. **Establish and assign roles and responsibilities.** I say to students: Each group member must accept responsibility for the work involved in achieving the ultimate goals of the group. As a group, decide what those roles are and who will fill those roles. Looking at the requirements of the assignment will help you determine what roles are necessary. You might identify successful teams of people (famous or not), identify the various roles and positions the team uses, and determine which roles might transfer to this project. These specific roles are required:

   a. *Recorder*—Records all ideas and suggestions in writing. This serves as a map of your progress as well as a resource for redirection.

   b. *Group Exit Slip Chair*—During the last 10 minutes of class, your team will stop working in order to clean up and to record the progress made, assign homework, and complete the intended plan for the next day. This team member submits these plans along with the team notes daily; the plans and notes serve as your exit slips.

   c. *Individual Self-Assessment*—Each student will assess your own contribution to the work of the team that day. This serves as your individual exit slip.

2. **Intra-team conflict.** If there is a disagreement or problem within a group, record in writing and bring to my attention the problem and every attempt to resolve the problem. Only if your team is unable to resolve the conflict will I mediate a solution.

3. **If your team finishes early.** If your group completes your research and presentation early, have alternative activities available. Unless you can contribute some guidance and assistance, you won't be interacting with other groups.

Troubleshooting tips:

Whether through an I-Search or a We-Search, educators can help students develop life skills that will serve them throughout their lifetimes. The more information students have about the expectations held by their teachers, the more successful they will be in attaining those expectations. Therefore, I clearly state in writing what individual behaviors are necessary for groups to be highly functioning and successful:

1. *Assignments:*

   a. Accepts responsibility for learning

   b. Solves complex problems

   c. Submits quality assignments

      i. Accurate

      ii. Precise

        iii. Neat

        iv. Legible

        v. Attends to requirements

        vi. On time

2. ***Behavior:***

   a. Follows classroom and team rules

   b. Focuses on task

   c. Exhibits self-control

   d. Accepts responsibility for behavior

   e. Respects others and the learning

   f. Collaborates positively with teammates and peers.

3. ***Preparation and Organization for Academic Work:***

   a. Considers the day and arrives to team completely prepared

   b. Locates materials readily

   c. Takes notes

   d. Utilizes an effective organizational system to enhance learning

   e. Uses class time effectively

   f. Seeks extra help when needed

4. ***Accountability For Learning:***

   a. Attends class regularly

   b. Participates in team discussions and activities

   c. Sets and monitors goals

   d. When necessary, seeks out teacher or other support independently.

One of the challenges of group work is the negative impact of absenteeism. When group members who are responsible for bringing work to the group are absent, precious time can be lost. Before beginning any group work, I make sure that all members within a group share contact information. One of the articles in every covenant behavior is that if a member of a group is unable to attend school, they are still responsible for getting any information or materials to the group to insure that his or her teammates can move forward.

Additional Time-Saving Strategies

What I Want to Know list. If teaching fluency in writing is not a major concern in your content area, the What I Want to Know section might be a list that includes a well-written guiding question and other, smaller questions, saving time in both the writing and the assessing of this section.

Stay in first person for *What I Learned*. At the What I Learned section, my eighth graders shift from writing in first person to writing in third person, moving from a more personal style to a formal academic format, though this is not necessary. Staying in the first person provides another opportunity for content area teachers to save some time, because first person tends to be less intimidating for middle school. For teachers whose focus is on content learned, having students continue to write in first person will reveal the lessons they have learned as a result of their research.

Another time saving approach for the What I Learned section would be to have each team author a formal presentation of their findings. The standards for both reading and writing can be easily assessed through a critical evaluating of a formal presentation.

Share instructional lessons with team. If you are part of a team or can teach parts of the required lessons for I-Search or We-Search, you can share the instructional responsibilities and workshop time among team teachers.

Reduce required drafts. If you choose to have students write each section, reducing the number of drafts required for the *What I Know, What I Want to Know,* and the *Research Journeys* will reduce the amount of time needed to write and assess papers. I would, however, suggest requiring more drafts for the What I Learned section, as this is a more formal piece and is the culmination of weeks of work.

Combine *What I Know and What I Want to Know*. Some students have suggested combining the What I Know and the What I Want to Know sections to save time and aid fluency, which has possibilities. Because identifying and articulating a dynamic guiding question is difficult even at the 8th grade level and requires a great deal of teacher guidance and support for many students, I recommend that students draft the *What I Know,* be guided through the development of questions, and then add to their first draft their *What I Want to Know.* They could then edit and revise both sections and submit it as one.

There are a number of ways that this unit of study can be adjusted to accommodate time and content challenges. The value of the *I-Search* or *We Search* paper cannot be overstated and its ability to address not only CCSS, but lifelong learning, is worth the investment.

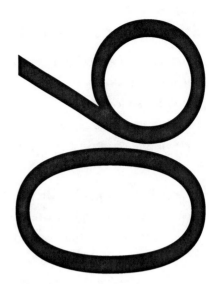

More 21st Century Skills Strategies

Give a man a fish and you feed him for a day.
Teach a man to fish and you feed him for a lifetime.
—Chinese Proverb

There is no doubt that current educational reform efforts have changed the landscape of public education in this nation. The NCLB legislation with its heavy emphasis on testing, has, for two decades, framed the discourse in educational reform around the teaching of content, often at the expense of the metacognitive process embedded in not only learning that content, but using that information to navigate and thrive in the world. Fortunately, a shift in that conversation is beginning to occur as it becomes more and more apparent that "content" can be elusive in a world that continually shifts and changes. The need to develop into lifelong learners has never been greater because of the speed at which the world changes. More than at any other time in our history, students will need to develop competencies in the skills needed to navigate these changes quickly.

Teachers can play a significant role in fostering lifelong learning by building into their pedagogical practice strategies that strengthen those skills, not only with regard to the I-Search process, but in fact, into any study focus within any discipline. Even adding some simple strategies to help students build stronger learning profiles can reap great rewards.

Strategies to Foster Growth in Each Domain of Lifelong Learning

Changing and Learning. Perhaps the most critical domain to success is Changing and Learning because it is closely tied to a student's belief in his or her ability to learn. Some students have failed for so long in school that they no longer believe that they can be successful. Before learning can take place, a student must believe in his or her ability to learn, so students must see evidence refuting any doubts they might hold. Strategies for encouraging students' belief in their abilities include:

- Recording what they know about a topic before starting the unit. For example, students might write what they know about the Cold War prior to studying that unit and again after they have completed it. Comparing their pre and post records can be a powerful illustration of students' ability to learn.

- Getting detailed feedback on assessments, emphasizing the student's strengths and how he or she can use that strength to overcome challenges

- Building a portfolio

- Incorporating self-assessment by comparing their past performance to their current level of accomplishment.

- Building a personal learning relationship with the teacher through a mentoring conference. Perhaps one of the most effective ways to strengthen this domain is a mentoring conference, in which the teacher can help a struggling student see the growth in learning that often goes unseen or unappreciated.

Critical Curiosity requires students to muster the courage to ask questions, so a safe environment in which students can take risks is needed. Additionally, fostering critical curiosity requires a balance of those asking the questions. In many classrooms throughout the country, teachers ask the predominant number of questions. While this might provide an excellent model initially, students must take the role of inquisitor if they are to fully engage in the learning. Strategies to encourage students to ask questions include:

- Students generate a list of facts about a topic rather than using a teacher-generated fact sheet. This simple reversal of responsibility places the onus on the students for asking the questions that lead to the important facts. It also shows possible false assumptions or associations they might have about the subject, giving the teacher the ability to clarify any misconceptions immediately.

- Before introducing a topic, ask students to record the questions they have about that topic. This helps pique their curiosity and provides them ownership of the lesson.

Meaning Making refers to the connections students make and the experiences from which they draw when they are attempting to make sense of the world. The ability to see patterns and connections between events and ideas is a critical skill for success. Strategies to encourage meaning making include:

- Students do the simple task of mind-mapping a topic. This gives them an opportunity to identify related pieces of information in a visual way and gives the teacher a chance to address any misconceptions that appear.

- Provide seemingly unrelated concepts or events and ask students to mind-map how they are connected. Once students have developed their own mind-maps, it can be very effective to then ask the students to step back, share their maps, and make connections and associations using the ideas and connections of others. Not only does this increase the knowledge base from which students can draw their conclusions, it also provides an opportunity to listen to other perspectives with an open mind.

- Ask students to describe how they arrived at a conclusion. This can help to model and explain the way in which others make meaning. For example, in literacy my students practice this when they are asked to explain why they interpreted a quote or text or defined a vocabulary word in the way that they did. They verbally trace their thought process that led them to their conclusion. While their interpretation may be flawed or their definition incorrect, the connections and path taken to those conclusions are often logical, providing the opportunity to identify value even in a "wrong" answer.

Creativity refers to the ability to be playful in one's learning and think in divergent ways. It is, therefore, heavily dependent on the level of safety a student feels within a classroom, especially at the middle level when young adolescents seek more than anything to conform. However, given the opportunity, this age group can demonstrate a gift for creativity. Strategies to encourage students' creativity include:

- In science, presenting students with a scientific problem and then asking them to create a path to solving that problem can generate all kinds of creative thoughts and experiments.

- In social studies, providing a "what if" scenario in which one event in history did not occur or is altered could generate some terrific results.

- In math, students could create a game that would teach a mathematical theorem or function to a younger group of students.

- In literacy, challenge students to write fractured fairy tales or six-word novels.

- In advisory, a repurposing unit in which each student brings in one item from home and, with three other students, creates something useful using all four items can push students to think in divergent ways while it provides a framework to also teach effective Learning Relationships.

Positive Learning Relationships are grounded in trust, so fostering and developing a classroom climate free of ridicule and judgment is imperative. Identifying the variety of learning needs within a classroom and clearly articulating the purpose of the class are essential cornerstones for promoting effective Learning Relationships. For example, students who need quiet in order to concentrate are often unaware that other students require noise in order to achieve the same level of concentration. Respecting and legitimizing each of those needs helps students to understand their peers' behaviors and often eliminates the negative judgments that are made in the absence of that knowledge. Strategies that build trust are:

- Direct discussions about how to meet the variety of learning needs within the classroom, including strategies and compromises, go a long way toward building a working community. Once trust is established, working with classmates that are not friends becomes less frightening.

- Require that all writing in class have at least one peer-edit before submission; randomly assign that editor to eliminate the propensity for students to go to their friends only. Entrusting your work to a stranger takes a great deal of trust, but it is a life skill. Everyone needs a good editor and infusing the practice of peer-editing for any written assignments provides a platform on which students can strengthen their Learning Relationships.

- When requiring students to work in groups, explicitly teach them how to work effectively in a group; it is not an innate ability.

- Construct group work in ways that teach the specific skill set needed to collaborate with others effectively.

Resilience, like Changing and Learning, is grounded in a student's emotional framework. As a result, both are by far the most important domains in lifelong learning with regard to shaping the decisions that learners make. According to the research, Resilience is also the domain that correlates most closely with academic success (Bruno, 2009). The more resilient an individual is, the more capable he or she is in developing the tenacity needed to overcome challenges and persevere. The research indicates that young children entering school are hugely resilient when they arrive, eager to try new things and undaunted by failed attempts. However, the longer a child is in school, the less resilient he or she becomes. Students quickly learn that being "right" is what is valued. The heavy emphasis on testing and the institutional practice of tracking send a powerful message to students about whom is best, and by default, who is not. The more children internalize these lessons, the less likely they are to take risks and the more likely they are to see their failings as evidence that there is something wrong with them. It is up to educators to combat these perceptions by shifting the focus of instruction from result to process. Reminding students of their strengths is often the best place to begin. Strategies for building resilience include:

- Encourage students to lean on their strengths when facing challenges to learning. If they are, for example, creative or critically curious, using these strengths to tackle an area of learning that presents a challenge will often help students persevere through difficult learning tasks. Indeed, knowing that they have specific strengths is often the first step to becoming more resilient.

- Build a supportive classroom culture. Encouragement from peers as well as teachers can go a long way to convincing a student to stick with it, so building a classroom culture that encourages students to support and cheer the hard work of others is often very effective in building resilience.

- Help students find their passion. There is no doubt that individuals are more resilient when they are very motivated to learn. Finding that individual passion within a student can be instrumental in developing the tenacity he or she will need in difficult leaning situations. Say, for example, you have a student who is passionate about softball and currently faced with a tough learning challenge. Help her to draw parallels between her ability to visualize the effort she invested to improve her batting average to what she needs to do to complete the learning task at hand.

- Point out examples of when he or she had overcame a learning challenge in the past.

Strategic Awareness involves executive function and ultimately enables students to take charge of their learning and succeed in less structured learning environments. At its heart *Strategic Awareness* is the ability to manage the processes involved in the learning and accomplish the desired outcomes. In this domain, students achieve self-efficacy and autonomy. Achieving independence in learning begins when students develop a reflective stance. Strategies for strengthening this domain are:

- After any unit of study, students take time to reflect on the outcomes they achieved for that unit and whether the processes they used were effective. They identify the choices they made and the resulting consequences of those choices. Coaching them to evaluate what went well and what, perhaps, did not, allows them to make adjustments to the way they work in order to attain the level of competence they seek. Reflection offers them the ability to build a repertoire of strategies that work for them.

- At the middle level, organization can be a challenge for many students, and becoming aware of their learning habits is essential to developing a successful system of organization.

- Modeling time management skills by sharing the process and the thinking behind the development of a unit of study can help students develop the capacity to see the big picture and then break it down into manageable pieces. Because all minds are not alike, a system of organization that insures a student keeps track of due dates and requirements must be specific to that student if it is to be successful. The more involvement a student has in the design and implementation of that system, the more likely he or she will succeed. Focusing on the process as opposed to the outcome is an essential piece of increasing Strategic Awareness.

By attending to and valuing the process of learning, teachers can more adeptly prepare their students for success in the 21st century. By making slight changes to pedagogical practice, educators can insure that their students develop into strong lifelong learners. This, in turn, will insure them a secure place in a global community, and allow for their voice to become a part of the world conversation.

Appendix FAQ-1
The 21st Century Classroom

A classroom in which the objective and focus include not only knowledge acquisition but also the desire to strengthen lifelong learning differs from more traditional classrooms in which the teacher is the keeper and dispenser of knowledge.

Function: In a 21st century classroom, the members of the class function as a democratic community. Both teachers and students are keenly aware of the purpose of education and their responsibility to insure the access to knowledge for all. Because the learning is dependent on active engagement as opposed to passive acceptance, there is often an energy and passion in the room. To the untrained eye, it may look chaotic, as students and teachers move seamlessly from being the "teacher" at one moment and the "student" in the next. Some students pursue the answer to one question, while others pursue the answer to another. Some students may work together and others alone, but all take ownership and responsibility for their learning.

Physical setting. The classroom may also differ from the traditional image of rows facing forward. A 21st century classroom ideally, has flexibility in environment and space to spread out the learning, so that information can be posted, stepped away from, viewed, shared, and revised. Abundant space is available for the expression and dissection of ideas. Additionally, access to information is seamless. If a student has a question, the resources needed to find the answer are available. Current technology is up-to-date, respected, used, and accessible to all.

Teacher-student relationship. Critical to any learning, whether traditional or constructivist, is the relationship between the students and the teacher. There is a level of mutual respect that honors the task at hand, celebrates the differences in the room, and fosters curiosity. A 21st century classroom differs from its predecessor in the value it places on the learning process over the end result—because in reality there is no true end result—the world keeps rapidly changing.

Student role in the 21st century classroom. The responsibility for meeting the current demands placed on schools does not rest solely on the shoulders of the teachers, however. Students in a 21st century learning environment need to become agents of their own learning, and that requires a shift in focus, skill, and time allocation. They would need to believe that being curious and creative are highly valuable and that through hard work they can learn. They would need to be resilient, flexible, and adaptable. They would need to approach their learning with an open mind and compassionate heart and be armed with multiple strategies to solve and address complex issues and problems. This would require students to invest time outside of the school day in their learning, a requirement that is more easily met if the work is authentic and personal.

In addition, students would need to be able to work well alone as well as together. Although teachers often assume students know how to work well with others, they often do not. Add to that construct the competitive framework that schools have infused into their structure, and very often the goal of the group is usurped by the goals of individuals seeking self-acknowledgment, praise, or a good grade. Collaboration is a very complex process with multiple strategies in communication, mediation, participation, appreciation, consideration, and more, all of which really require direct instruction and the abandonment of personal glory. In a very competitive world, group work exposes the hypocrisy of our educational system—the world needs all of us to work together *and* if you don't work hard enough to be ranked in the top 10% of your class, you can kiss that position at Harvard good-bye. Every teacher who has ever assigned a group project has seen the fallout of these two opposing messages. There are those students who love group work, because they know someone else will do the heavy lifting. Others dread it, because they need to control the outcome in order to protect their academic standing; therefore, they do the heavy lifting. Still others would love to collaborate, but find themselves with others who do not, and then feel stuck with doing all the work. Without honest discussions and direct instructions, a product will almost always be produced, but the opportunity to shift mind-set and develop valuable lifelong skills will be lost. Students would not only need to know how to navigate interpersonal skills, but also need to pursue competence in technology and literacy, not for its own sake, but to be used to communicate and share their ideas and understandings. In order to achieve this, they would need to partner with their teachers and parents and other caring adults and become active and engaged learners and their own best advocates. In other words, they need to become fearless and we need to create the environment in which that can safely happen.

Appendix 1-1
A Parent's Introduction to the I-Search Paper

The following is a sample of what a letter to parents might include.

Dear Parent or Guardian,

In the past when I've taught the eighth graders to research, they understood little about the research process and focused largely on the format of the finished product. As a result, their research papers often lack substance and depth. To address this problem and help them develop a deep appreciation for the value and the workload of true research, my students will be writing an **I-Search** paper, a paper with 5 distinct sections. I will describe the paper in hopes that you will support your student's efforts to learn to research because it is a lifelong skill they will need.

The **I-Search** paper shows the process that people go through when they want to learn more about a topic. It is based on the idea that good research comes from a personal desire to learn something, so it is essential that the chosen topic is one about which the researcher is passionate.

In the first section, *What I Know*, students record what they already know about their topics; they do this prior to doing any serious research. Note that in this section *the information does not need to be accurate*. As a matter of fact, it often is not. Students will learn a great deal from realizing how their preconceived notions and opinions obscure reality and truth.

The second section, *What I Want to Know*, addresses the questions that the researcher has about his or her topic. Identifying all the questions a student has about a topic paves the way to identifying their guiding question, which is the road map for their research.

After your child has written an approved guiding question, they begin the actual research. During the *Research Journey* your child will identify a minimum of 6 sources from which they will seek answers to questions about their topic. They will write a summary of 3 of those sources: one book or journal, one website, and one personal interview. They will learn research strategies to help them find the information they seek and to evaluate the validity and trustworthiness of the sources they choose.

In the fourth section, *What I Learned*, students synthesize the information from their sources and describe what they had learned about their chosen topic. Students will learn how to structure a paper according to ideas rather than sources, write a compelling introduction with a sound thesis, and conclude with a clear statement of the importance of the topic studied. Once the final What I Learned section is written, they will include a brief paragraph in which they will reflect on the process and how it has shaped them as learners and researchers. They will return to the 1st person and share their thoughts on the effectiveness of the I-Search in helping them grow as learners.

The final section will be the *Works Cited* page. The students will learn the proper MLA format of citing their sources on a formal works cited page and understand the relationship between in-text citations and that page.

This is a long process and, while time will be given in class for much of the research and writing, your child will be required to research, revise, draft, and edit every night for homework in order to remain on schedule. A calendar of due dates and assignments are posted on my website, though your child should be able to share with you were they are in the process when asked.

As always, if you have any questions or would like more information concerning this unit of study, please don't hesitate to send me an email or give me a call.

Sincerely,
Dr. Bruno

Appendix 1-2
The 7 Domains of Lifelong Learning and I-Search

1. **Critical Curiosity** is the ability to look deeper into a topic and to want to know more is what research is all about. You will be challenged to draw from your critical curiosity not only to identify a topic that is of great interest to you, but also to maintain that interest throughout the I-Search project.

2. The **Learning Relationships** domain speaks to the value of your relationships with others and their ability to serve as resources for your learning. Through the I-Search process of peer-editing; discussions with experts in the field; requesting assistance of librarians and teachers; and conversations with peers, parents, and family friends, you will develop skills that will help to develop learning relationships that are meaningful and rich.

3. The research process requires you to express **Creativity** when new knowledge challenges you to look at old ways of thinking. The necessity of synthesizing new information and forming new perspectives as you consider the ways that these relate to the larger question of "repairing the world" will require you to think in different, creative ways.

4. Throughout the process of producing an I-Search paper, you will demonstrate **Strategic Awareness** as you follow specific processes and time lines and read critically, manage new information, and construct new knowledge. You will identify and apply many strategies to meet the unit requirements. If you struggle in this area, focus on what you need to do and identify specific strategies that will help you strengthen this domain.

5. In all learning, **Meaning Making**, the ability to connect new knowledge to what is already known to develop a deeper and broader foundational understanding of an issue, is critical. By definition, research is an act of Meaning Making. In the What I Have Learned section, you describe how information discovered in your Research Journeys supports, changes, and expands what you wrote in your What I Know section. By consciously drawing connections between old and new information, you can strengthen your skills in this area.

6. For those who need to strengthen their **Resilience**, there is comfort in knowing that no one knows everything. The process of research requires the researcher to repeatedly figure out what more there is to learn about a topic. The ability to seek answers to questions indicates a strong and confidant learner. Throughout the *I-Search* process, you learn that the ability to recognize what is unknown drives intelligence. Students who lack resilience often shut down when they perceive their work as inferior or "wrong." If you are one of these students, then the *I-Search* paper will present you with multiple opportunities to build your resilience. You will be asked to consult others throughout the research process through interviews and peer-editing which require you to confidently learn from others and recognize the recommendations offered for improvement not as personal failures, but rather as ways you can grow in your knowledge.

7. Finally, the *I-Search* process requires hard work. If done well, it provides tangible proof that through hard work and guided focus you can become smarter. By comparing the *What I Know* section to the *What I Have Learned* section, you will have the evidence you need to demonstrate that you are capable of **Changing and Learning**.

Appendix 1-3
CCSS Related to I-Search

Reads to Comprehend Informational Text Grade 8

Key Ideas and Details

1. Cite the textual evidence that most strongly supports an analysis of what the text says explicitly as well as inferences drawn from the text.

2. Determine a central idea of a text and analyze its development over the course of the text, including its relationship to supporting ideas; provide an objective summary of the text.

3. Analyze how a text makes connections among and distinctions between individuals, ideas, or events (e.g., through comparisons, analogies, or categories).

Craft and Structure

4. Determine the meaning of words and phrases as they are used in a text, including figurative, connotative, and technical meanings; analyze the impact of specific word choices on meaning and tone, including analogies or allusions to other texts.

6. Determine an author's point of view or purpose in a text and analyze how the author acknowledges and responds to conflicting evidence or viewpoints.

Integration of Knowledge and Ideas

9. Analyze a case in which two or more texts provide conflicting information on the same topic and identify where the texts disagree on matters of fact or interpretation.

Writing Standards 8th Grade

Text Types and Purposes:

2. Write informative/explanatory texts to examine a topic and convey ideas, concepts, and information through the selection, organization, and analysis of relevant content.

   2a. Introduce a topic clearly, previewing what is to follow; organize ideas, concepts, and information into broader categories; include formatting (e.g., headings), graphics (e.g., charts, tables), and multimedia when useful to aiding comprehension.

   2b. Develop the topic with relevant, well-chosen facts, definitions, concrete details, quotations, or other information and examples.

   2c. Use appropriate and varied transitions to create cohesion and clarify the relationships among ideas and concepts.

   2d. Use precise language and domain-specific vocabulary to inform about or explain the topic.

   2e. Establish and maintain a formal style.

   2f. Provide a concluding statement or section that follows from and supports the information or explanation presented.

3. Write narratives to develop real or imagined experiences or events using effective technique, relevant descriptive details, and well-structured event sequences.

    3a. Engage and orient the reader by establishing a context and point of view and introducing a narrator and/or characters; organize an event sequence that unfolds naturally and logically.

    3b. Use narrative techniques, such as pacing, description, and/or reflection, to develop experiences, events, and/or characters.

    3c. Use a variety of transition words, phrases, and clauses to convey sequence, signal shifts from one time frame or setting to another, and show the relationships among experiences and events.

    3d. Use precise words and phrases, relevant descriptive details, and sensory language to capture the action and convey experiences and events.

    3e. Provide a conclusion that follows from and reflects on the narrated experiences or events.

Production and Distribution of Writing

4. Produce clear and coherent writing in which the development, organization, and style are appropriate to task, purpose, and audience. (Grade-specific expectations for writing types are defined in standards 1–3 above.)

5. With some guidance and support from peers and adults, develop and strengthen writing as needed by planning, revising, editing, rewriting, or trying a new approach, focusing on how well purpose and audience have been addressed. (Editing for conventions should demonstrate command of Language standards 1–3 up to and including grade 8.)

6. Use technology, including the Internet, to produce and publish writing and present the relationships between information and ideas efficiently as well as to interact and collaborate with others.

Research to Build and Present Knowledge:

7. Conduct short research projects to answer a question (including a self-generated question), drawing on several sources and generating additional related, focused questions that allow for multiple avenues of exploration.

8. Gather relevant information from multiple print and digital sources, using search terms effectively; assess the credibility and accuracy of each source; and quote or paraphrase the data and conclusions of others while avoiding plagiarism and following a standard format for citation.

9. Draw evidence from literary or informational texts to support analysis, reflection, and research.

Listening and Speaking

Presentation of Knowledge and Ideas

4. Present claims and findings, emphasizing salient points in a focused, coherent manner with relevant evidence, sound valid reasoning, and well-chosen details; use appropriate eye contact, adequate volume, and clear pronunciation.

5. Integrate multimedia and visual displays into presentations to clarify information, strengthen claims and evidence, and add interest.

6. Adapt speech to a variety of contexts and tasks, demonstrating command of formal English when indicated or appropriate.

Appendix 2-1
Finding a Researchable Topic

1. **Identify A Topic.**

   a. State your topic idea as a question. For example, if you are interested in finding out about child labor, you might pose the question, "Is there or has there ever been child labor in the United States?"

   b. Identify the main concepts or keywords in your question. In this case they are "Child labor" and "United States".

2. **Test Your Topic.**

   a. Test the main concepts or keywords in your topic by looking them up in the appropriate background sources or by using them as search terms.

   b. * If you are finding *too much* information and too many sources, narrow your topic by using the 'and' operator: child labor and United States, for example.

   c. * Finding *too little* information may indicate that you need to broaden your topic. For example, look for information on child labor throughout the world, rather than just the United States. Link synonymous search terms with or: child labor or child exploitation. Shortening search terms also broadens the search and increases the number of items you find.

3. **Finding Background Information**

   a. Once you have identified the main topic and keywords for your research, find one or more sources of background information to read. These sources will help you understand the broader context of your research and tell you in general terms what is known about your topic. The most common background sources are encyclopedias and dictionaries. Class textbooks also provide background information.

   b. *TIP: EXPLOIT BIBLIOGRAPHIES* - Read the background information and note any useful sources (books, journals, magazines, etc.) listed in the bibliography at the end of the encyclopedia article or dictionary entry. The sources cited in the bibliography are good starting points for further research.

   c. Write down these sources in your notes to build a list of possible resources. Remember that many of the books and articles you find will themselves have bibliographies. Check these bibliographies for additional useful resources for your research. By using this technique of routinely following up on sources cited in bibliographies, you can generate a surprisingly large number of books and articles on your topic in a relatively short time.

Parent Letter and Topic Approval Form

Dear Parent or Guardian,

We are beginning our first major writing project for the year: The I-Search paper. You received a letter earlier introducing this unit of study, but in case you didn't receive that, the I-Search paper is a visual representation of the process that people go through when they want to learn more about a topic. Ask your child to share the 'Buying the Car' metaphor to explain exactly what an I-Search paper is. For more information, please go to my website for an explanation, the rationale, and the objectives for this unit of study. http://lbruno.d41teachers.org or send me an email. I will be happy to answer any questions you might have.

At its core, the I-Search paper is fueled by a person's desire to learn more about something. Because this unit of study will span 6 weeks, your child has been asked to select a topic for which they passionately would like to learn more about and one that is related to the theme of "Tikkun Olam," a Hebrew phrase meaning "Repair the World." In class we have been exploring ideas for topics of study and your child should have created a list of issues for which he or she holds some interest. The I-Search paper follows a natural course of inquiry where your child is actively involved in the process and will be seeking information not only from traditional sources such as books and articles, but from people who have some expertise in the topic being searched. It is imperative, therefore, that you be aware of the chosen topic and approve of that topic. Your child has been encouraged to discuss his or her topics of interest with you and may solicit you for additional ideas.

I have asked your child to record below the five top topics he or she is interested in pursuing and to discuss each with you. Your child should be able to explain to you why these topics interest him or her. Please take some time to sit down with your scholar and discuss the topics listed and then come to a decision about which topic he or she will research. Remember, it must be a topic about which they care deeply and one with which you approve. If you are, for whatever reason, not happy with your child's choice, please, through a conversation with your child, identify two or three topics you would support and record those below.

As always, thank you for your support.   ~ Dr. Bruno

My Top Five Topics:

Topic	Reason for Interest
1.	
2	
3.	
4.	
5.	
The Topic I have Chosen is: _____	

Appendix 2-3
Cornell Notes

Cornell notes is a template designed to assist students in identifying the key topics/ideas and essential details related to that topic or idea. A 1-2 inch column is created by drawing a vertical line down the left side of a piece of paper in which the key idea or topic is written. In the wider column to the right, the significant details related to that topic or idea is recorded. At the end of the note taking session (or for homework) students will then summarize their understanding of the information. A sample model of Cornell notes follows.

Dr. Bruno
I-Search
Nov. 6 2012   (1)

Topic	Be passionate about it
Requirements	- 1st person (I) - What I Know - Questions - Talk to someone who knows my topic - Read what experts say about my topics (books, articles, web) - Share what I learn - Bibliography - Works cited
Format What I Know	- 1-2 # - experience, background why I'm interested
What I Want to Know	- Questions - Guiding question - approved by Dr. Bruno Very Important - Keeps focus & leads to sources
Research Journey	- MLA citation at top of summary - 1st # - How I found source & found it credible - Summarize what I learned from source - Conclusion - Share thoughts & opinions - 4 Sources = 1 book or article; 1 website; 1 interview +other
What I Learned	- Write about what I learned - Introduction - thesis (question restated as thesis) - How new knowledge has changed me

Appendix 2-4
Pacing Yourself Through the Project

Pacing Yourself Through this Project

The Eight Steps to Success

As far as the writing is concerned, each section of this paper will require the following steps. I call them the **Eight Steps to Success**. Following the **Eight Steps to Success** takes a minimum of 3 days per paper, often longer, *for the writing portion and does not include the time it takes to formulate the questions, find the sources, read those source, take notes on those source, and think about the information,* all of which can add many days to the process.

1. Initial draft
2. Self-edit
3. 2nd draft
4. Peer-edit
5. 3rd draft
6. Self-edit
7. Polished Draft
8. Self-assessment using rubric

How Long Will it Take?

Experience has shown that following these guidelines will help you make a successful plan for your research: :

1. Plan for the **What I Know** section to take 3-4 days.

2. Writing a researchable question(s) can be difficult. Plan to spend a day or two working and reworking the question(s) before beginning the *Eight Steps to Success* for the **What I Want to Know** section. (3-4 days)

3. The **Research Journey/Works Cited** will, by far, take the bulk of your time. In this section you will report out on the information you discover. This is where you will spend much of your time searching, critically reading, and synthesizing new knowledge with old knowledge. Questions will be answered and new questions will arise. A GREAT DEAL OF TIME WILL BE SPENT BEFORE YOU EVEN BEGIN WRITING. Allow a minimum of 10 –12 days to complete the write up of 3 sources. Remember, each source requires:

   a. MLA citation

   b. A description of how you discovered this source

   c. The process you used to evaluate the source

   d. A summary of the information in the source

   e. A description of what questions were answered and what questions were raised; what knowledge was confirmed, what knowledge was challenged, and what new knowledge was discovered.

4. The **What I Have Learned** section also requires a lot of time, as this is the point at which you think deeply about what you have learned and communicate that to your reader. You will support your opinions and conclusions with evidence from your sources and cite those sources in your writing. Additionally, you will share with the reader how you have grown as a learner as a result of having gone through the I-Search project. Allow 3-4 days to complete this section.

5. The **Work Cited**, if the Research Journey is done correctly, is a matter of simply copying and pasting, or exporting as a Word document from EasyBib and should take about 5–20 minutes.

6. Your **Reflection** paragraph should take another 20 to 30 minutes. In this paragraph you return to 1st person and share your thoughts about the I-Search process. What did you learn about the art of research? What was valuable? Tell the story of your experience as a learner as you moved through the process.

Appendix 2-5
Scheduling the *I-Search* Project

Due Dates

The final *What I've Learned* section of the **I-Search** paper will be due on December 12th. Note the due dates for other sections of the paper below and put them in your passport. There are multiple steps to this paper and it is essential that you plan out and pace yourself through this project. While I know scheduling is challenging, this good practice for high school and any important project you will take on in real life. To help you, the due dates for each section of your paper follow.

Signed Topic Approval	November 8th
Section 1: What I Know	November 13th
Research Question: Approval	November 14th
Section 2: What I Want to Know	November 16th
Section 3: Research Journey	
Source #1:	November 26th
Source #2:	November 29th
Source #3:	December 4th
Section 4: What I've Learned	December 12th
Section 5: Works Cited	December 12th

After entering these due dates in your assignment notebook, think seriously about what steps are involved and when you will have time to complete those steps while you work toward the final product. **While you will be given the opportunity to work on this paper in class, much of the work will need to be accomplished outside of the school day.** Plan accordingly.

Appendix 2-6
Student Checklist

Student Checklist

Format Requirements:
Typed (initial draft is exempt from this requirement)
Double spaced
Font: Times New Roman / Ariel
Font size: 12
Title: Section title, aligned left, Title case, and bolded
Header: Name, period, Research Topic, date Aligned right
Footer: Page numbers, centered

(1) **Parent Letter** – due Nov. 8
☐ Topic Approval / Letter of Consent from Parent

(2) **What I Know** – due Nov. 13
☐ Initial draft
☐ Self-edit
☐ 2nd draft
☐ Peer-edit
☐ 3rd draft
☐ Polish-edit
☐ Polish Draft
☐ Rubric

(3) **Research Question** – due Nov. 14
☐ Question approved

(4) **What I Want to Know** – due Nov. 16
☐ The Big Question
☐ Initial draft
☐ Self-edit
☐ 2nd draft
☐ Peer-edit
☐ 3rd draft
☐ Polish-edit
☐ Polish Draft
☐ Rubric

(5) **Research Journey #1** – due Nov. 26
☐ Work citation
☐ Notes/Summary of source
☐ Book/Journal

☐ Interview
☐ Web-site
☐ Other
☐ Initial draft
☐ Self-edit
☐ 2nd draft
☐ Peer-edit
☐ 3rd draft
☐ Polish-edit
☐ Polish Draft
☐ Rubric

(6) **Research Journey #2** – due Nov. 29
☐ Work citation
☐ Notes/Summary of source
☐ Book/Journal
☐ Interview
☐ Web-site
☐ Other
☐ Initial draft
☐ Self-edit
☐ 2nd draft
☐ Peer-edit
☐ 3rd draft
☐ Polish-edit
☐ Polish Draft
☐ Rubric

(7) **Research Journey #3** – due Dec. 4
☐ Work citation
☐ Notes/Summary of source
☐ Book/Journal
☐ Interview

☐ Web-site
☐ Other
☐ Initial draft
☐ Self-edit
☐ 2nd draft
☐ Peer-edit
☐ 3rd draft
☐ Polish-edit
☐ Polish Draft
☐ Rubric

(8) **What I Learned/Work Cited/ Reflection** – due Dec. 12th
☐ Initial draft
☐ Self-edit
☐ 2nd draft
☐ Peer-edit
☐ 3rd draft
☐ Polish-edit
☐ Polish Draft
☐ Rubric
☐ Sources in proper format
☐ Alphabetical order

(9) **Polished Copy in U-drive** – TBA
☐ What I Know
☐ What I Want to Know
☐ Research Journey
☐ What I Learned
☐ Work Cited
☐ Check Format
 o Single-spaced
 o Title – centered, bold
 o Author – centered
 o Section Headings (left), bold

Appendix 2-7
What I Know Standards-Based Rubric

Write **NARRATIVES** to develop real or imagined experiences or events using effective technique, relevant descriptive details, and well-structured event sequences.

WC3a. Engage and orient the reader by establishing a context and point of view and introducing a narrator and/or characters; organize an event sequence that unfolds naturally and logically.			
M	P	NM	My lead is interesting and sets up what I know about my topic.
M	P	NM	I describe clearly and logically the story of how I became interested in this topic.
WC3b. Use narrative techniques, such as pacing, description, and/or reflection, to develop experiences, events, and/or characters.			
M	P	NM	I Use effective literary devices/techniques to show my enthusiasm for this topic.
M	P	NM	I pace my reader through what I know about my topic, lingering on the important points where appropriate.
M	P	NM	I reflect on my experiences and share my thoughts and feelings about the topic.
WC3c. Use a variety of transition words, phrases, and clauses to convey sequence, signal shifts from one time frame or setting to another, and show the relationships among experiences and events.			
M	P	NM	My transitions lead my reader seamlessly through my story.
M	P	NM	I use a variety of clauses and transitions to signal shifts in time and experiences.
M	P	NM	I effectively communicate the relationship between experiences that have developed my interest in this topic.
WC3d. Use precise words and phrases, relevant descriptive details, and sensory language to capture the action and convey experiences and events.			
M	P	NM	I use words that precisely communicate my thoughts and feelings about this topic.
M	P	NM	My word choice accurately captures my interest and shares my experiences and the events that have contributed to my interest in this topic.
M	P	NM	My word choice create the intended emotion and supports the purpose of the piece.
WC3e. Provide a conclusion that follows from and reflects on the narrated experiences or events.			
M	P	NM	My conclusion justifies the reason I have chosen this topic.
M	P	NM	My conclusion reflects on why this topic is of interest for me.
M	P	NM	My conclusion convinces my reader that this topic is of interest to me.

Production and Distribution of Writing

WC4. Produce clear and coherent writing in which the development, organization, and style are appropriate to task, purpose, and audience.

M	P	NM	
M	P	NM	My idea is focused and aligns with the guidelines of the specific genre.
M	P	NM	My introduction aligns with the guidelines of the specific genre and draws the reader in.
M	P	NM	The sequence of ideas/information/events is logical and effective providing clarity to the reader.
M	P	NM	My transitions are effective and provide cohesion, moving the reader seamlessly through the piece.
M	P	NM	My conclusion drives home the 'So What' of the piece.
M	P	NM	Word choice is precise and concise and appropriate for the specific genre.
M	P	NM	Sentence fluency creates a rhythm and provides fluency.
M	P	NM	Spelling and grammar rules are followed.
M	P	NM	My voice communicates my enthusiasm and commitment to my topic.

WC5. With some guidance and support from peers and adults, develop and strengthen writing as needed by planning, revising, editing, rewriting, or trying a new approach, focusing on how well purpose and audience have been addressed. (Editing for conventions should demonstrate command of Language standards 1–3 up to and including grade 8.)

M	P	NM	
M	P	NM	I have a minimum of 1 Self-edit sheet completed.
M	P	NM	I have a minimum of 1 Peer-edit sheet completed.
M	P	NM	I have incorporated peer suggestions for improvement.
M	P	NM	I have revised my writing for ideas, organization, word choice, sentence fluency, conventions, and voice producing a minimum of 4 drafts.
M	P	NM	I have edited for my personal writing goals.

Appendix 2-8
What I Know Self-Edit

Standards	Yes	No	If Yes–Example/Evidence If No–Suggestions for Improvement
Do I use effective writing techniques and relevant descriptive details to present the information?			
Does my writing engage and orient the reader by establishing a context and point of view?			
Is my writing well organized, presenting information and sequencing events and/or details in a natural and logical way?			
Have I used precise words and phrases, relevant descriptive details, and sensory language to convey my interest in the topic?			
Does my conclusion follow logically and reflect on my reasons for wanting to research this topic?			
Is my writing clear and coherent?			
Are the development, organization, and style of writing appropriate to the purpose of the assignment and audience?			
Have I developed and strengthened my writing by considering peer and adult suggestions?			
Does my writing reflect attention to planning, revising, editing, and rewriting?			
As an author, have I focused on how well my purpose and audience have been addressed?			
Have I formatted my paper correctly following the established requirements for font, font size, alignment, spacing, as well as requirements for header and footer?			
Have I edited for my personal writing goals?			

Appendix 2-9
What I Know Peer-Edit

Standards	Yes	No	If Yes–Example/Evidence If No–Suggestions for Improvement
Does the author use effective writing techniques and relevant descriptive details to present the information?			
Does the writing engage and orient you as the reader by establishing a context and point of view?			
Is the writing well organized, presenting information and sequencing events and/or details in a natural and logical way?			
Has the author used precise words and phrases, relevant descriptive details, and sensory language to convey his or her interest in the topic?			
Does the conclusion follow logically and reflect on the reasons for why the author wants to research this topic?			
Is the writing clear and coherent?			
Are the development, organization, and style of writing appropriate to the purpose of the assignment and you as the audience?			
Does the writing reflect attention to planning, revising, editing, and rewriting?			
Is there evidence that the author focused on his or her purpose and considered his or her audience?			
Does the formatting of the piece follow established requirements including font, font size, alignment, spacing, and appropriate information in the header and footer?			
As the peer-editor, do you feel the author invested enough time in the writing and editing process, by producing an effective and well-written piece?			

Appendix 2-10
Student Example of *What I Know*

Biomedical Engineering
By Claire Wild

What I Know:

The world of science can be quite obscure at times. One look at the word "deoxyribonucleic acid," (DNA) and many people immediately go blank. These people are also the people who can't see past the obvious careers in science like a veterinarian, chemist or surgeon. If you dig deeper into the growing science textbook, you will realize just how many different occupations are available. There are basic categories, and then there are specific types of those categories, such as biomedical engineering (BME.) The word itself seems intimidating (and so it might be,) but this area of science alone is one of the fastest progressing occupations for future medical advancements. BME is at its peak at the present time, for more and more programs are gaining speed and many colleges are investing in more ways to promote this discipline of study.

The basic idea of engineering was introduced to me through a seminar in downtown Chicago. At the event specifically based around getting young girls interested in engineering, we watched a montage explaining exactly what an engineer does. The effects were instantaneous. Although at the time I thought that the event was focused on girls younger than I, I found that my true interest had been uncovered. After a mere four hours of exposure to crafts, professional representatives, and the particular details of the occupation, I had completely changed around my idea of a golden future.

Having interests in art and science, I was not sure what career would capture both of my interests. In my brain, the diorama of my future had always shown me becoming a pediatrician and just having art as a hobby. After this seminar however, those ideas plus engineering were thrown into a melting pot and mixed together until I came out with a final product that combined both art and science; biomedical engineering. This individual field of engineering focuses on the creation of vaccines, medical imaging such as ultrasound, medical devices, and artificial limb design and function. BME radically interests me because it combines both my creative interests and science.

In today's society, the need for engineers is on the rise. It is considered one of the careers of the future due to its rapidly evolving technology and information at hand. No matter how obscure it seems, engineering can be the perfect balance of creativity and science. In my research journey, I hope to explore the nooks and crannies of BME and soon figure out the possibilities of the future. Will there be a cure for cancer? Could we ever make an artificial limb that is seamless with the human body? As this powerful career rises to its peak, the possible medical discoveries could infinitely change the treatments given to patients of all sickness intensities and maybe even the population of America.

Appendix 2-11
What I Want to Know Standards-Based Rubric

WC2. Write **INFORMATIVE/EXPLANATORY** texts to examine a topic and convey ideas, concepts, and information through the selection, organization, and analysis of relevant content.

WC2a. Introduce a topic clearly, previewing what is to follow; organize ideas, concepts, and information into broader categories; include formatting (e.g., headings), graphics (e.g., charts, tables), and multimedia when useful to aiding comprehension.

M	P	NM	I have written an effective thesis statement.
M	P	NM	My introduction previews my topic and the main question I have about that topic.
M	P	NM	My sentence fluency communicates the intended message.
M	P	NM	I use sophisticated transitions that move my reader through my inquiry seamlessly.

Production and Distribution of Writing

WC4. Produce clear and coherent writing in which the development, organization, and style are appropriate to task, purpose, and audience.

M	P	NM	My primary guiding question is well focused and stated.
M	P	NM	My introduction clearly establishes the topic and the interest I have in that topic.
M	P	NM	The sequence of information (statements) and questions is logical and effective providing clarity to the reader and creating an appropriate rhythm when read.
M	P	NM	Transitions are effective and provide cohesion and aid in creating that rhythm.
M	P	NM	My conclusion revisits my primary guiding question and communicates my desire to learn more about this topic.
M	P	NM	My word choice is precise and concise and effectively communicates the questions I have and the direction I intend to take during my research.
M	P	NM	My sentence fluency contributes to cohesion and fluency of piece, creating a readable rhythm.
M	P	NM	I follow the rules for conventions and are appropriate for this assignment.
M	P	NM	My voice is used to enhance the piece and convinces my audience that I have a true interest in learning more about my topic.

			WC5. With some guidance and support from peers and adults, develop and strengthen writing as needed by planning, revising, editing, rewriting, or trying a new approach, focusing on how well purpose and audience have been addressed. (Editing for conventions should demonstrate command of Language standards 1–3 up to and including grade 8.)
M	P	NM	I identified the primary role I intend to take when researching (advocate, reporter, educator).
M	P	NM	I considered and incorporated the feedback I received from my peers and adults who assisted me in the process of writing this piece.
M	P	NM	I revised my writing for ideas, organization, word choice, sentence fluency, and voice producing a minimum of 4 drafts.
M	P	NM	I polished my writing, editing for conventions an my personal writing goals.

RE - Research to Build and Present Knowledge

			RE7. Conduct short research projects to answer a question (including a self-generated question), drawing on several sources and generating additional related, focused questions that allow for multiple avenues of exploration.
M	P	NM	I formulated a list of questions that reflected my personal interest in this topic.
M	P	NM	I sought information from others to assist in the development and revision of my questions.
M	P	NM	My questions are divergent and flexible enough to allow for discovery.

Appendix 2-12
What I Want to Know Self-Edit

Standards	Yes	No	If Yes—Example/Evidence If No—Suggestions for Improvement
Do I introduce my topic clearly, previewing what is to follow by organizing my ideas and questions into broader categories and/or appropriate limitations?			
Have I written a focused guiding question and generated additional related, focused questions that allow for multiple avenues of exploration?			
Do I help my reader understand my inquiry by using relevant, well-chosen questions and adequate definitions, concrete details, and/ or other information and examples?			
Do I produce clear and coherent writing and balance statements and questions in order to create a readable rhythm?			
Does my conclusion follow logically, revisit the guiding question, and reflect on the reasons that I want to research this topic?			
Is my writing clear and coherent?			
Does my writing reflect attention to planning, revising, editing, and rewriting?			
Have I clearly focused on my purpose and stayed true to my identified role (advocate, reporter, educator)?			
Does my formatting of the piece follow established requirements including font, font size, alignment, spacing, and appropriate information in the header and footer?			
Did I invest enough time in the writing and editing process, as is evident by the quality of writing?			

Appendix 2-13
What I Want to Know Peer-Edit

Standards	Yes	No	If Yes–Example/Evidence If No–Suggestions for Improvement
Does the author introduce his or her topic clearly, previewing what is to follow by organizing his or her ideas and questions into broader categories and/or appropriate limitations?			
Has the author written a focused guiding question and generated additional related, focused questions that allow for multiple avenues of exploration?			
Does the author aid in your understanding of his or her inquiry by using relevant, well-chosen questions and adequate definitions, concrete details, and/or other information and examples?			
Did the author produce clear and coherent writing in which the author balances statements and questions and creates a readable rhythm?			
Does the conclusion follow logically, revisit the guiding question, and reflect on the reasons for why the author wants to research this topic?			
Is the writing clear and coherent?			
Does the writing reflect attention to planning, revising, editing, and rewriting?			
Is there evidence that the author focused on his or her purpose and stayed true to his or her (advocate, reporter, educator)?			
Does the formatting of the piece follow established requirements including font, font size, alignment, spacing, and appropriate information in the header and footer?			
As the peer-editor, do you feel the author invested enough time in the writing and editing process, by producing an effective and well-written piece?			

Appendix 2-14
Developing a Research Question

1. **Consider Your Readers** Brainstorm a response to the following questions. While freewriting your answers to the following questions, keep the needs and interests of your readers in mind:

   a. Why will my readers care about this issue?

   b. What will my readers want or need to know about this issue?

   c. What do my readers already know about this issue?

   d. What do I want my readers to learn about the issue?

   e. If I am trying to persuade my readers of something, how easily will they be persuaded?

2. **Select a Role** Consider what role you will *primarily* adopt throughout the research—such as reporter, advocator, or educator—as a writer. Essentially, you need to consider how the different roles would allow you to accomplish your purpose as a writer. Below is a list of three possible roles. These roles are not mutually exclusive—you might adopt one role or another at different points in the paper.

   • Advocate – a person who speaks for and promotes a point of view often for those who cannot speak for themselves, but not necessarily

   • Reporter – a person who presents the information that exists, keeping bias to a minimum

   • Educator – a person who is presenting information for the purpose of educating their audience about a specific topic

3. **Generate Potential Research Questions** Read your freewrite and identify main curiosities that hold your interest. Then consider your readers and the possible roles you might adopt. Begin drafting possible research questions. Use the words what, why, when, where, who, and how as starting points for your questions. You might also use the words would, should, or could.

4. **Select a Primary Research Question** After you review the information from the first three steps, begin to group your questions into like categories. For example some questions might reference the politics of an issue, while others might address the economics. This will help you to identify your main area of interest concerning your topic. Draft a guiding research question, one that will get to the heart of what you would like to learn about your topic. Your guiding research question will most likely be a combination of at least two categories.

5. **Narrow or Broaden the Scope of Your Research Question**

   a. Narrowing a broad question: The trick to writing a good guiding question is to write a question that is neither too narrow nor too broad. For example, "What are the causes of World War II?" would be too broad a guiding question. However, "What political factors led to the American involvement in World War II?" helps to narrow the focus of your research. To narrow a broad guiding question, try adding a limitation such as location, industry, time, or political, social, or economic factors.

   b. Broadening a narrow question: Narrow questions do not allow for much research. For example, "Who invented the radio?" is easily answered in one or two sentences. A researchable question might be "How did radio change the face of America in the 20th century?"

DEVELOPING A RESEARCH QUESTION: Worksheet

1. **Freewrite on the back of this paper.** *(See "Consider Your Readers")*

   _____

   _____

   _____

2. **Select a Role:** *(circle one)*   *Advocate*   *Reporter*   *Educator*

3. **Generate Potential Research Questions:** *(a minimum of 10)*

   1. _____

   2. _____

   3. _____

   4. _____

   5. _____

   6. _____

   7. _____

   8. _____

   9. _____

   10. _____

4. **Identifiable categories:**

   1. _____   2. _____

   3. _____   4. _____

5. **Select a Primary Question:**

   _____

   _____

6. **Narrow the Scope of Your Research Question:** (Take your time here —this will make or break your research. Review the questions above and identify categories {i.e. political, social, economic issues). Think about limitations that would help frame and control your search {i.e. location - U.S as opposed to the world). Using these broader categories and as well as these limitations, try to craft a question that frames your research well, giving you enough to research, but not too much!) This is very difficult and I will certainly help, but not until you've given it your best shot :o)!

   _____

   _____

7. **Dr. Bruno's Approval:** (And the Primary Guiding Question is . . . (drum roll, please :o)

   _____

   _____

_____   _____
Dr. Bruno's initials   Student initials

Appendix 3-1
Research Journey Standards-Based Rubric

CI. Reads to Comprehend Informational Text
Key Ideas and Details

CI1. Cite the textual evidence that most strongly supports an analysis of what the text says explicitly as well as inferences drawn from the text.			
M	P	NM	I effectively summarize what the source says explicitly.
M	P	NM	I interpret the text both explicitly and implicitly.
M	P	NM	I select and use multiple pieces of text evidence that effectively support my interpretation and summary.
CI2. Determine a central idea of a text and analyze its development over the course of the text, including its relationship to supporting ideas; provide an objective summary of the text.			
M	P	NM	I identify and state clearly the central idea of source.
M	P	NM	I identify the most relevant supporting details from the text.
M	P	NM	I draw relationships between the central idea and those supporting details.
M	P	NM	I synthesize all the information within the source to determine a cohesive message.
M	P	NM	I write a clear summary of that source, stating the message and supporting the interpretation of that message with text evidence .
CI3. Analyze how a text makes connections among and distinctions between individuals, ideas, or events (e.g., through comparisons, analogies, or categories).			
M	P	NM	I identify how the text compares and contrasts ideas/individuals/events.

Craft and Structure

CI4. Determine the meaning of words and phrases as they are used in a text, including figurative, connotative, and technical meanings; analyze the impact of specific word choices on meaning and tone, including analogies or allusions to other texts.			
M	P	NM	I identify new vocabulary or common vocabulary used in an unfamiliar way.
M	P	NM	I recognize how specific word choices refine meaning.
M	P	NM	I identify how the negative, positive, or neutral connotations implicit in the word choice and context communicates the author's meaning and tone.

CI6. Determine an author's point of view or purpose in a text and analyze how the author acknowledges and responds to conflicting evidence or viewpoints.			
M	P	NM	I articulate the author's point of view and/or purpose using evidence and word choice from the source.
M	P	NM	I consider opposing points of view and/or alternative purposes if presented.
M	P	NM	I identify evidence and word choice within the text that indicates the author's consideration of opposing viewpoints or recognize that such evidence is missing.
WC2. Write **INFORMATIVE/EXPLANATORY** texts to examine a topic and convey ideas, concepts, and information through the selection, organization, and analysis of relevant content.			
WC2a. Introduce a topic clearly, previewing what is to follow; organize ideas, concepts, and information into broader categories; include formatting (e.g., headings), graphics (e.g., charts, tables), and multimedia when useful to aiding comprehension.			
M	P	NM	I have written the MLA citation above the source.
M	P	NM	I tell how I found this sources including the key words used.
M	P	NM	I tell how I determined the credibility of the source.
WC2b. Develop the topic with relevant, well-chosen facts, definitions, concrete details, quotations, or other information and examples.			
M	P	NM	I select strong and relevant evidence/facts to support, inform, and/or explain.
WC2c. Use appropriate and varied transitions to create cohesion and clarify the relationships among ideas and concepts.			
M	P	NM	I use sophisticated transitional devices to strengthen relationship between ideas and concepts.
WC2d. Use precise language and domain-specific vocabulary to inform about or explain the topic.			
M	P	NM	I use precise language and vocabulary specific to the topic to inform the reader, incorporating new vocabulary into my summary.
WC2e. Establish and maintain a formal style.			
M	P	NM	I maintain formal writing that adheres to the requirements of the assignment.
WC2f. Provide a concluding statement or section that follows from and supports the information or explanation presented.			
M	P	NM	I share what I learned from this source.
M	P	NM	I identify what questions from my WIWK were answered and any new questions that were raised.
M	P	NM	I share my interpretation and opinion about the value of the information found in this source and how it has informed my research.

Production and Distribution of Writing

WC4. Produce clear and coherent writing in which the development, organization, and style are appropriate to task, purpose, and audience. (Grade-specific expectations for writing types are defined in standards 1–3 above.)

M	P	NM	
M	P	NM	I clearly articulate the idea(s) and content found in my source.
M	P	NM	The sequence of ideas/information/events is logical and provides clarity to the reader.
M	P	NM	My transitions are effective and provide cohesion.
M	P	NM	My conclusion identifies the questions this source has answered, reflected on how the source addressed my personal interest, and identified additional questions, if any, that were raised.
M	P	NM	My word choice is precise and concise and supports clarity.
M	P	NM	My sentence fluency contributes to cohesion and fluency.
M	P	NM	I follow the rules for conventions.
M	P	NM	My voice is identifiable and connects effectively with audience.

WC5. With some guidance and support from peers and adults, develop and strengthen writing as needed by planning, revising, editing, rewriting, or trying a new approach, focusing on how well purpose and audience have been addressed. (Editing for conventions should demonstrate command of Language standards 1–3 up to and including grade 8.)

M	P	NM	
M	P	NM	I considered and incorporated the feedback I received from my peers and adults who assisted me in the process of writing this piece.
M	P	NM	I revised my writing for ideas, organization, word choice, sentence fluency, and voice producing a minimum of 4 drafts.
M	P	NM	I polished my writing, editing for conventions an my personal writing goals.

RE. Research to Build and Present Knowledge			
RE7. Conduct short research projects to answer a question (including a self-generated question), drawing on several sources and generating additional related, focused questions that allow for multiple avenues of exploration.			
M	P	NM	I have identified the questions I had about my topic that this source has answered.
M	P	NM	I have reflected on how this source addressed my personal interest.
M	P	NM	I have articulated the relevance of this source to my stated research journey.
M	P	NM	I have identified additional questions, if any, that this source has raised.
RE8. Gather relevant information from multiple print and digital sources, using search terms effectively; assess the credibility and accuracy of each source; and quote or paraphrase the data and conclusions of others while avoiding plagiarism and following a standard format for citation.			
M	P	NM	I used and revised effective search terms to identify and locate appropriate sources.
M	P	NM	I determined the credibility and accuracy of this source and eliminated questionable resources.
M	P	NM	I effectively summarized the information found in this source.
M	P	NM	I identified questions that were answered and acknowledging the information that generated further questions.
M	P	NM	I wrote the citation for this source in MLA format.
M	P	NM	I used online tools to construct the MLA citation when possible or used the MLA guidelines to construct the citations when online tools were not available.

Research Journey Self-Edit

Standards	Yes	No	If Yes–Example/Evidence If No–Suggestions for Improvement
Do I effectively and explicitly describe the main idea(s) in the source?			
Do I share what background knowledge I used to help me interpret the ideas in the source?			
Do I objectively summarize the text by sharing what is said explicitly and sharing what is implied?			
Do I select and use multiple pieces of text evidence to support my interpretation and summary of the text?			
Do I explain how that evidence supports the central idea?			
Do I identify and provide context and meaning for the reader of the pertinent individuals, organizations, events, ideas, etc. in the text?			
Do I categorize and organize the information in a way that promotes understanding for my reader?			
Do I define new vocabulary related to my topic for my reader?			
Do I honestly convey and support with text evidence the author's tone, point of view, and purpose?			
Do I identify and evaluate each argument and/or claim made by the author?			
Do I acknowledge in my summary opposing points of view or missing evidence?			

(Continued)

Appendix 3-2
Research Journey Self-Edit *(continued)*

Standards	Yes	No	If Yes–Example/Evidence If No–Suggestions for Improvement
Do I have the MLA citation above the source?			
Do I tell how I found and evaluated the credibility of the source?			
Do I effectively introduce my reader to the central ideas in the source setting up a foundational understanding of what is to come?			
Do my transitions clarify the relationships among ideas and concepts and move my reader from one idea to the next smoothly?			
Do I use precise language and topic-specific vocabulary to inform about or explain the ideas found in this source?			
Does my conclusion reflect on how the source addressed my personal interest, answered my question(s), and identified new questions that were raised?			

Appendix 3-3
Research Journey Peer-Edit

Standards	Yes	No	If Yes–Example/Evidence If No–Suggestions for Improvement
Does the author effectively and explicitly describe the main idea(s) in the source?			
Does the author share what background knowledge he or she used to help him or her interpret the ideas in the source?			
Does the author objectively summarize the text by sharing what is said explicitly and sharing what is implied?			
Does the author select and use multiple pieces of text evidence to support his or her interpretation and summary of the text?			
Does the author explain how that evidence supports the central idea?			
Does the author identify and provide context and meaning for the reader of the pertinent individuals, organizations, events, ideas, etc. in the text?			
Does the author categorize and organize the information in a way that promotes understanding for his or her reader?			
Does the author define new vocabulary related to his or her topic for the reader?			
Does the author honestly convey and support with text evidence the author of the text's tone, point of view, and purpose?			
Does the author identify and evaluate each argument and/or claim made by the text's author?			

(Continued)

Research Journey Peer-Edit *(continued)*

Standards	Yes	No	If Yes—Example/Evidence If No—Suggestions for Improvement
Does the author acknowledge in his or her summary opposing points of view or missing evidence?			
Does the author have the MLA citation above the source?			
Does the author tell how he or she found and evaluated the credibility of the source?			
Does the author effectively introduce his or her reader to the central ideas in the source setting up a foundational understanding of what is to come?			
Do his or her transitions clarify the relationships among ideas and concepts and smoothly move the reader from one idea to the next?			
Does the author use precise language and topic-specific vocabulary to inform or explain the ideas found in this source?			
Does the author's conclusion reflect on how the source addressed his or her personal interest, answered his or her question(s), and identified new questions that were raised?			

Appendix 3-4
Example of *Research Journey*

By Perry Zumbrook

Levitin, Daniel J. *This Is Your Brain on Music: The Science of a Human Obsession.* New York, NY: Dutton, 2006. Print.

In an effort to find out if there is a biological reaction that takes place within the brain when humans listen to music, I searched online to find suitable sources from which I could gather scientific data. My original search came under the heading of "physical effects from listening to music." Eventually, I discovered that the wealth of information I was looking for came under the search hit "emotional effects from listening to music" and "how music affects our brain." Interestingly, one name kept popping up in almost every website I searched. This one particular name was also referenced on several online interviews on talk radio programs. That name was Daniel Levitin, a neuroscientist and even more surprising, former record producer. It was at this point that I googled Levitin's name and found a series of books he had written, from which I selected *This Is Your Brain on Music.* Fortunately I was able to get a copy of Levitin's book from the Glen Ellyn Library the next day.

Although elated that I had come across a resource that might help answer my question as to whether there is a biological or chemical reaction that takes place when listening to music, I needed to confirm that Daniel Levitin was a credible source to quote. My fears were set to rest when I learned that Daniel Levitin was, and still is, a professor who runs the Laboratory for Musical Perception, Cognition, and Expertise at McGill University in Quebec, Canada, where he holds the Bell Chair in the Psychology of Electronic Communications. Professor Levitin just also happened to have been an accomplished musician, sound engineer, and record producer in Los Angeles and New York before becoming a neuroscientist. To date, he has written numerous scientific journals, as well as books and music trade magazine articles. Highly regarded by individuals in both the scientific community and music industry, I felt confident that I had found a credible source to research and gather information from for my I-Search paper.

As my goal was to discover a connection between the music we listen to and the physical and emotional reactions we have as a result from that music, I knew I was looking for some pretty complex information. In *This Is Your Brain on Music,* Professor Levitin goes into great detail explaining just why music has been a critical step in human evolution. Levitin makes clear that the music we think is tugging at our heartstrings is really only a physical reaction to what is actually going on in our head. In his own words, Levitin describes this action as an "exquisite orchestration of brain regions" which is engaged in a "precision choreography of neurochemical uptake and release." Music is what helps Levitin understand how everything works in the human brain. It is Levitin's belief, and current argument, that music has been fundamental to the success of our species.

Levitin's theory is as follows: when we listen to music, our brains engage in a highly sophisticated computational task. Our brain not only recognizes an internal representation of sound, it also experiences some degree of pleasure from that sound. In that moment, an area of the brain called the cerebellum is activated. Originally it was thought that the main purpose of the cerebellum was to coordinate the movement and timing of our bodies. Through much research, however, Levitin has proven that it also has a more complicated purpose, which is registering emotions; particularly the way we experience joy or pleasure from the rhythm or beat of a piece of music. Our ears not only send a signal to our auditory cortex, the region of the brain that processes sound, it also transmits straight to the cerebellum which keeps time in the brain, synchronizing the beat. From this point on, the brain is playing a game that it loves to play. Our brain finds pleasure in guessing and predicting when beats will occur. As Levitin hypothesized, the brain becomes highly excitable when a song violates the expected beat in some surprising way. Levitin's research showed that our cerebellum finds great joy when forced to adjust to stay synchronized. The cerebellum, however, is just one of a large number of systems that are activated when we listen to music. The frontal lobe, a higher order region that processes musical structure, is also affected as well as the mesolimbic system, which Levitin explains is "involved in arousal, pleasure, and the transmission of opiods and production of dopamine." This explains why we can feel a variety of such deep emotions when we listen to music. This reaction is the same euphoric effect experienced when using a highly powerful drug. Levitin writes, "As a tool for arousing feelings and emotions, music is better than language." This having been said, music can bring people to an emotional state of wanting to create good in order to continue the high they experience from the music they love.

The lesson I learned from this resource was that there is a biological effect when listening to music. It is that affect which brings about emotion, passion, and purpose. My question now is, how do we get from feeling good about music, to doing something good within our own communities as well as globally? What is the link between music and lyrics and moving the masses to do something charitable? I hope to answer that question as I try to understand the origin of music and the part it has played in our history? I am also curious if there is significance to those findings in our lives today.

Appendix 3-5
Website Evaluation Guide

Website Rubric: How reliable is the information on this website?

Website	Trustworthy	Questionable
1. Is the site hosted by a credible provider and residing in a 'trustworthy' domain? (circle the one that applies: .edu = education; .gov = government; .org = organization; .com = commercial; .net = internet)	☐ .edu ☐ .org ☐ .gov	☐ .com ☐ .net
2. Does the stated mission posted on the site imply a bias?	☐ No	☐ Yes
3. Do the people and/or organizations listed in the About Us raise questions about the credibility or bias of the source?	☐ No	☐ Yes
4. Was the website updated recently?	☐ Yes	☐ No
5. Are the site's authors/founders experts in the subject? (Do they have any credentials or experience on the topic?)	☐ Yes	☐ No
6. Are there links and references to other websites, resources, and experts that corroborate this information?	☐ Yes	☐ No
7. Are there any "dead links", or links to "moved pages"?	☐ No	☐ Yes
8. Do the site's authors/founders have other publications with credible sites and publishers?	☐ Yes	☐ No
9. Is contact information provided and does the place/e-mail exist and work?	☐ Yes	☐ No
10. Is the site professional (grammar and typing errors are not present or very minimal)?	☐ Yes	☐ No
11. Does the site present highly biased visuals (e.g. racist statements, derogatory remarks, and emotional language)?	☐ No	☐ Yes
12. Do the images support the stated facts?	☐ Yes	☐ No
13. Do large companies you know of advertise on the site?	☐ Yes	☐ No

Appendix 3-6
Whipping Up *Works Cited*

If you have followed instructions and kept track of your sources on EasyBib, creating your Works Cited page is a snap. Follow these simple instructions and attach the printed page to the *What I Learned* section of your paper.

1. Log on to EasyBib.

2. Click on your Bibliography.

3. Delete from the list any sources you did not use in your research.

4. Click *Export or Print* button.

5. Select *Print as Word Doc.*

6. *Click Here to Download.*

7. Print your *Works Cited* page.

8. Staple to the back of your *Works Cited.*

If you have not kept a record of all your sources on EasyBib, your life has just gotten more difficult. You will need to enter them into EasyBib before following the steps above.

Appendix 3-7
The Art of Interviewing

Determining the purpose. Before arranging an interview, first determine why you are conducting the interview and what you hope to learn from the interview. State your purpose in such a way that the person you are interviewing can understand it and determine if they can be of assistance to you. Ask yourself: *what type of information can an interview with this person provide me about my topic that I can't get from other sources?*

Structuring the interview. *Questions* are the heart of any interview. Create an Interview Guide (see below) that includes all the questions you intend to ask during the interview. The Guide will serve as a roadmap to help you to gather the information you seek and to establish a positive relationship with your interviewee.

Phrasing Questions. How you phrase questions during the interview is important in getting the information you need. Follow these simple guidelines:

- o Be specific and precise.
- o Avoid language that might offend or insult interviewee.
- o Make sure the question is important to your stated purpose.
- o Phrase questions so they are simple, clear requests for limited amounts of information.
- o Do not ask multiple questions, such as, "How and why did you begin your photography career?" or "What movies have you seen lately? How would you rate them and why?"
- o Order your questions in a logical way.
- o Do not ask questions that the interviewee cannot answer.
- o Do not ask questions that insult the interviewee.

Types of Questions. An important part of preparing your interview guide is asking the appropriate types of questions. Questions may be *primary* or *secondary*; *open-ended* or *closed-ended*; *neutral, leading,* or *loaded*. There are also *special types* of questions listed below.

1. An **open-ended question** encourages a full, meaningful answer using the subject's own knowledge and/or feelings. Open-ended questions also tend to be more objective and less leading than closed-ended questions. THESE TYPES OF QUESTIONS WILL GET YOU THE MOST INFORMATION BUT REQUIRE SERIOUS LISTENING!!!!!

2. A **closed-ended question** encourages a short or single-word answer. Limit these in your interview.

3. **Primary questions** are often the first ones you ask, and they are usually planned. They can stand alone out-of-context; they make sense without follow-up explanation of what information is needed.

4. **Secondary questions** are often follow-up questions to something the interviewee has said. They attempt to get more information and are often unplanned because the questioner thinks of them due to answers already given.

Design questions for the Interview Guide that will help your interviewee give complete, thoughtful, and clear answers. Base your questions on the interview's purpose, what you know about the topic, and what you know about the interviewee. Careful preparation increases the likelihood of a productive interview.

Conducting the interview. The interview process is:

1. Begin by thanking the interviewee for taking the time to speak with you.

2. Tell the interviewee the purpose of your interview.

3. First ask an open-ended question.

4. Use respectful body language: Make eye-contact, face the interviewee, nod your head, and indicate that you are a part of the conversation.

5. Refer to your guide, but don't hesitate to change the plan if your interviewee reveals interesting information that you would like to know more about. Practice active listening (make a conscious effort to hear and understand). Remember, the interview is a conversation.

6. Take notes, but do not allow the note taking to cause your interviewee to sit for long periods of time waiting for you to finish writing. You can ask your interviewee whether he or she minds if you record the conversation, which eliminates the need for taking notes. If he or she does mind, you cannot record the conversation.

7. At the end of the interview, be sure to ask a clearinghouse question such as, *"Is there anything else you would like to share with me that you think is important for me to know?"*

8. Be sure to send a short thank you note to your interviewee after the interview.

Tips for successful Skype interviews. A few things to keep in mind when conducting Skype interviews are:

- Look at the camera, not the screen to make direct eye contact (you will be tempted to watch yourself or your interviewer).

- Make sure there are no side conversations by members in the group

- Pick a quiet place and close the door to prevent interruptions

- Be sure to adjust the Skype audio ahead of time to make sure you can both hear and be heard clearly.

- Don't tinker with computer during call; no tapping on keyboard

- Close other programs on your computer; make sure all other windows are closed (especially if they make noise).

- Address any technical problems immediately; if there are many blips or glitches, stop the call and redial.

Appendix 3-8
Interview Guide

Interviewer: _____ Interviewee: _____

Topic: _____ Dr. Bruno's approval: _____

Purpose of Interview: Identify the reason you are conducting the interview and what you hope to learn from the interviewee. To help you write the purpose of your interview, answer the following questions:

1) What type of information can an interview provide about your topic that you can't get from other sources?

2) What do you hope to learn from this interview? Write your introduction here:

Request for an interview: When requesting an interview, share with the interviewee why you are contacting him or her, where you got his or her name, and how long you anticipate the interview to last (15 minutes). If your potential interviewee agrees to the request, ask where and when it would be convenient for the interviewee (not you). If you are contacting the interviewee via email, please draft the text of the email here (use the back if necessary). If you will be speaking to the interviewee, please draft what you intend to say here.

Questions: Write a variety of primary questions, making sure you have mostly open-ended questions. Remember, this is just a guide. Secondary questions arise during the interview. Close the interview asking whether the interviewee would like to share any more information. Avoid leading and loaded questions and take enormous care not to insult your interviewee.

Primary Questions:

    1.

    2.

    3.

    4.

    5.

    6.

    7.

    8.

    Clearinghouse question:

Closing: Be sure to thank the interviewee for taking the time to speak with you.
YOU MUST WRITE A THANK YOU NOTE AFTER THE INTEVIEW.

Appendix 4-1
What I Learned Standards-Based Rubric

Reads to Comprehend Informational Text

CI1. Cite the textual evidence that most strongly supports an analysis of what the text says explicitly as well as inferences drawn from the text.			
M	P	NM	I effectively summarize what the source says explicitly.
M	P	NM	I interpret the text both explicitly and implicitly.
M	P	NM	I select and use multiple pieces of text evidence that effectively support my interpretation and summary.

CI9. Analyze a case in which two or more texts provide conflicting information on the same topic and identify where the texts disagree on matters of fact or interpretation.			
M	P	NM	Identify authors' points of view and purposes in each text.
M	P	NM	Select evidence used in each text to support the claims regarding authors' points of view and purposes.
M	P	NM	Match conflicting pieces of information used within each text.
M	P	NM	Evaluate whether evidence is factual or interpretive.

Writer's Craft

WC2. Write **INFORMATIVE/EXPLANATORY** texts to examine a topic and convey ideas, concepts, and information through the selection, organization, and analysis of relevant content.			

WCa. Introduce a topic clearly, previewing what is to follow; organize ideas, concepts, and information into broader categories; include formatting (e.g., headings), graphics (e.g., charts, tables), and multimedia when useful to aiding comprehension.			
M	P	NM	My introduction introduces my topic and goes from general to specific.
M	P	NM	My thesis statement clearly previews what I discuss in my paper.
M	P	NM	My formatting meets the requirements of the assignment.

WC2b. Develop the topic with relevant, well-chosen facts, definitions, concrete details, quotations, or other information and examples.			
M	P	NM	Each paragraph has a clearly stated topic sentence that previews what is discussed within that paragraph.
M	P	NM	I clearly present the central ideas or concepts found in my research.
M	P	NM	I select strong and relevant evidence/facts to support, inform, and/or explain the central ideas or concepts.
M	P	NM	I am careful to cite within the text the source from which those ideas or concepts were obtained.

WC2c. Use appropriate and varied transitions to create cohesion and clarify the relationships among ideas and concepts.			
M	P	NM	I use academic transitions that clearly identify the source of the ideas and concepts disucussed.

WC2d. Use precise language and domain-specific vocabulary to inform about or explain the topic.			
M	P	NM	My word choice is precise and results in concise writing.
M	P	NM	I define for my reader any terminology or ideas that are topic specific.

WC2e. Establish and maintain a formal style.			
M	P	NM	I avoid using the universal 'you' and/or 'we'.
M	P	NM	I write in active voice and avoid passive voice.

WC2f. Provide a concluding statement or section that follows from and supports the information or explanation presented.			
M	P	NM	I summarize the significance of the major ideas, concepts, and/or conclusions presented in my paper.
M	P	NM	I revisit my thesis.
M	P	NM	I provide an extension by sharing my interpretation and opinion about the value of the information found in this source.

Production and Distribution of Writing

WC4. Produce clear and coherent writing in which the development, organization, and style are appropriate to task, purpose, and audience.			
M	P	NM	I clearly articulate the idea(s) and content found during my research.
M	P	NM	The sequence of ideas/information/events is logical and provides clarity to the reader.
M	P	NM	My word choice is precise and concise and supports clarity.
M	P	NM	My sentence fluency contributes to cohesion and fluency.
M	P	NM	I follow the rules for conventions.

WC5. With some guidance and support from peers and adults, develop and strengthen writing as needed by planning, revising, editing, rewriting, or trying a new approach, focusing on how well purpose and audience have been addressed. (Editing for conventions should demonstrate command of Language standards 1–3 up to and including grade 8.)			
M	P	NM	I considered and incorporated the feedback I received from my peers and adults who assisted me in the process of writing this piece.

M	P	NM	I revised my writing for ideas, organization, word choice, sentence fluency, and voice producing a minimum of 4 drafts.
M	P	NM	I polished my writing, editing for conventions an my personal writing goals.

RE8. Gather relevant information from multiple print and digital sources, using search terms effectively; assess the credibility and accuracy of each source; and quote or paraphrase the data and conclusions of others while avoiding plagiarism and following a standard format for citation.

M	P	NM	I used and revised effective search terms to identify and locate appropriate sources.
M	P	NM	I determined the credibility and accuracy of this source and eliminated questionable resources.
M	P	NM	I effectively summarized the information found in this source.
M	P	NM	I identified questions that were answered and acknowledging the information that generated further questions.
M	P	NM	I wrote the citation for this source in MLA format.
M	P	NM	I used online tools to construct the MLA citation when possible or used the MLA guidelines to construct the citations when online tools were not available.

Appendix 4-2
What I Learned Self-Edit

Standards Do I ...	Yes	No	If Yes–Example/Evidence If No–Suggestions for Improvement
effectively and clearly summarize main idea(s) and concepts of my sources?			
cite the ideas and concepts correctly, so the reader understands whose ideas they are?			
support the ideas/concepts presented with evidence drawn from my sources?			
introduce my topic in an introduction that goes from general to specific, ending with my thesis statement?			
preview the central ideas and concepts in the topic sentence of each paragraph?			
give evidence from a variety of sources to support each central idea or concept?			
explain the significance of these ideas and concepts?			
use academic transitions to identify my sources and move the reader smoothly through my paper?			
identify and evaluate each argument and/or claim made by the author?			
use precise words, so that my writing is concise?			
define any terminology or provide context for specific information?			
avoid using the universal 'you' or 'we'?			
use active voice?			
summarize the major ideas/concepts, revisit my thesis, and extend my thinking by addressing the relevance of what I have learned in my conclusion?			

Appendix 4-3
What I Learned Peer-Edit

Standards Does the author:	Yes	No	If Yes–Example/Evidence If No–Suggestions for Improvement
effectively and clearly summarize the main idea(s) and concepts of the sources?			
cite the ideas and concepts correctly, so that the reader understands whose ideas they are?			
support the ideas/concepts presented with evidence drawn from the sources?			
introduce the topic in an introduction that goes from general to specific, ending with a thesis statement?			
preview the central ideas and concepts in the topic sentence of each paragraph?			
give evidence from a variety of sources to support each central idea or concept?			
explain the significance of these ideas and concepts?			
use academic transitions to identify sources and move the reader smoothly through the paper?			
identify and evaluate each argument and/or claim made by the author?			
use precise words, so that the writing is concise?			
define any terminology or provide context for specific information?			
avoid using the universal 'you' or 'we'?			
use active voice?			
summarize the major ideas/concepts, revisit the thesis, and extend the thinking by addressing the relevance of what has been learned?			

Appendix 4-4
Summarizing and Synthesizing

Source: _____ Date: _____

Facts	Opinion	Changes in Thinking

Appendix 4-5
Key Phrases for Citing Evidence

Change the verbs:

Callahan . . . believes, claims, states, identifies, agrees, disagrees, explores, holds, argues, defines, contends, responds, supports, summarizes, raises the question, . . . etc.

Change the preposition:

As Callahan states in his book, *"Education And The Cult Of Efficiency,"*

According to Callahan, author of . . .,

In Dewey's 1916 essay, Democracy and Education, he summarized . . .

In addition, Howard claims . . .

When asked if . . ., Smith responded . . .

As stated earlier . . .

Some researchers . . .

Change the nouns:

Several researchers . . . (support, reveal, agree, disagree, corroborate, etc.)

The literature . . . (supports, reveals, agrees, disagrees, corroborates, etc.)

The authors . . .

This study describes . . .

Appendix 5-1
Presentation Software

Slide show applications you may want to consider in addition to PowerPoint are Prezi, Google Presentation, and Glogster Online Poster. Although PowerPoint may have the most features, some other programs allow you to "save as" to other formats; some live in the cloud; and some are free. Here are some of the features of the programs.

PowerPoint (Word) /Keynote (Mac)

o   Has transitions

o   Uses slides as its format

o   Allows students to insert music and sounds.

o   Allows for adding hyperlinks.

o   Allows students to embed movies and pictures.

Prezi

o   It is cloud-based, so you cannot save your own copy of the presentation except in your account online. The desktop version of Prezi allows you to save a copy on your personal desktop.

o   Instead of building a linear slide show, it allows students to create a large canvas of grouped topics and then flow in and out of each freely while presenting. This allows presenter to show context because it can zoom out to show the entire presentation.

A student must be 13 to have an account.

o   Educators can have a free, upgraded account.

o   Requires a strong Internet connection as it is highly graphic

o   Allows students to link to YouTube videos and upload pictures

o   Does not allow hyperlinks

o   Takes a bit of finesse and resilience to use

o   Because it requires a sign-in and kids forget ID's and passwords, you may want to have them use the school's if you have access.

Google Presentation

• Cloud-based application, so it does not have the bells and whistles of PowerPoint or Keynote

• Very useful for teams who are collaborating virtually to build a presentation because team members can make edits live, at the same time

• Has animation effects, transitions, and drawing tools

• Easily imports from and exports to a variety of file types, like PowerPoint

• Free to use with a Google account

Glogster–Online poster

- Best used with younger students
- Works well to embed hyperlinks, audio, and video
- Students can create a text box that scrolls
- Use to limit amount of text—its one screen limits the amount of information
- Requires both teacher and student to sign-in
- Glogster Edu requires teachers to set up a class in order for students to use it
- A cost is associated with it

Appendix 5-2
Presentation Rubric

LS4. Present claims and findings, emphasizing salient points in a focused, coherent manner with relevant evidence, sound valid reasoning, and well-chosen details; use appropriate eye contact, adequate volume, and clear pronunciation.

M	P	NM	Introduction defines topic, tells why it was of interest, and presents guiding question.
M	P	NM	Presentation identifies integral points and presents them clearly.
M	P	NM	Presentation provides evidence that supports claims and findings.
M	P	NM	The evidence and support used includes specific details that speak to the audience.
M	P	NM	Presentation provides valid reasoning and explanation in support of claims and findings.
M	P	NM	Presentation engages and interests the audience.
M	P	NM	Conclusion punches home the 'so what.'
M	P	NM	Conclusion provides the audience with reasons why they should care and information about where they might go for more information.
M	P	NM	Presenter uses effective eye-contact and body language to support the tone of the presentation.
M	P	NM	Presenter enunciates clearly, including domain specific or technical vocabulary.
M	P	NM	Presenter projects voice to reach all members of the audience.

LS5. Integrate multimedia and visual displays into presentations to clarify information, strengthen claims and evidence, and add interest.

M	P	NM	Selected presentation method is effective for the topic.
M	P	NM	Presentation presents findings or information by integrating a variety of media (i.e. diagrams, charts, illustrations, video, multimedia, and all available technology).
M	P	NM	Selected media appeals to intended audience.

LS6. : Adapt speech to a variety of contexts and tasks, demonstrating command of formal English when indicated or appropriate.

M	P	NM	Presenter appropriately adjusts register (formal, semi-formal, informal) dependent on context or specific task.

FEEDBACK:

References

Brown, D. (2006). It's the curriculum, stupid: There's something wrong with it. *Phi Delta Kappa.* Retrieved from http://www.pdkintl.org/kappan/k_v87/k0606bro.htm

Bruno, L. (2009). *Lifelong learning characteristics and academic achievement of eighth-grade students: Lessons for educators in preparing students for global citizenship.* Walden University. Ann Arbor, MI. ProQuest LLC. UMI 3379880

Crick, R. D., Broadfoot, P., & Claxton, G. (2004, November). Developing an effective lifelong learning inventory: The ELLI Project. *Assessment in Education, 11*(3), 247–272.

Dean, M. J. (May 2006). Can we get beyond letter grades? *Educational Leadership. 63*(8). Retrieved from http://www.ascd.org/publications/educational-leadership/may06/vol63/num08/Can-We-Get-Beyond-Letter-Grades%C2%A2.aspx

Dewey, J. (January 1897). My pedagogic creed. *School Journal. 54,* 77–80. Retrieved from http://dewey.pragmatism.org/creed.htm

Fish, K., & McLeod, S. (2007, February 19). *Did You Know? Shift Happens!* YouTube. Retrieved from http://www.youtube.com/watch?v=pMcfrLYDm2U

Gardner, H. (2004). How education changes: Considerations of history, science, and values. In M.M. Suárez-Orozco & D. B. Qin-Hillard (Eds.), *Globalization: Culture and education in the new millennium.* (pp. 235–258). Los Angeles: University of California Press.

Hargreaves, A. (2003). *Teaching in the knowledge society: Education in the age of insecurity.* New York: Teachers College Press.

Holt, M. (2002). It's time to start the slow school movement. *Phi Delta Kappa International.* Retrieved from http://www.pdkintl.org/kappan/k0212hol.htm

Kohn, A. (2004). *What does it mean to be well educated? And more essays on standards, grading and other follies.* Boston, MA: Beacon Press.

Lemann, N. (1999). *The big test: The secret history of the American meritocracy.* New York: Farrar, Straus and Giroux.

Macrorie, Ken (1988). *The I-Search paper.* Portsmouth, NH: Boynton-Cook/Heinemann.

Mondale, S., & Patton, S. (Eds.). (2001). *School: The story of American public education.* Boston: Beacon Press.

National Commission on Excellence in Education. (1983). *A nation at risk: The imperative for educational reform: A report to the Nation and the Secretary of Education, United States Department of Education.* Washington, D.C.: National Commission on Excellence in Education.

National Governors Association Center for Best Practices, Council of Chief State School Officers. (2010). *Common Core State Standards for English Language Arts.* Washington, D.C: Author.

Pope, D. (2001). *Doing school: How we are creating a generation of stressed out, materialistic, and miseducated students.* New Haven, CT: Yale University Press.

Ravitch, D. (2010). *The death and life of the great American school system: How testing and choice are undermining education.* New York: Basic Books.

Rothstein, R., Wilder, T., & Jacobsen, R. (2007, May). Balance in the balance. *Educational Leadership, 64*(8), 8–14.

Springer, M. (2006). *Soundings: A democratic student-centered education.* Westerville, OH: National Middle School Association.

Suárez-Orozco, M. M., & Qin-Hillard, D. B. (Eds.). (2004). *Globalization: culture and education in the new millennium.* Los Angeles: University of California Press.

Tew, M., Crick, R. D., Broadfoot, P., & Claxton, G. (2004). *Learning power: A practitioner's guide.* Manchester, UK: Lifelong Learning Foundation.

U.S. Department of Education. (2011, December 15). *No Child Left Behind Legislation and Policies.* Retrieved from http://www2.ed.gov/policy/elsec/guid/states/index.html

Walker, D. (2002), Constructivist leadership standards, equity, and learning-weaving whole cloth from multiple strands. In *The constructivist leader* (pp. 1–33). Oxford, OH: National Staff Development Council.

Wormeli, R. (2006). *Fair isn't always equal.* Westerville, Ohio: National Middle School Association.

Zhao, Y. (2006). Are we fixing the wrong things? *Educational Leadership. 63*(8), 23–31.

CPSIA information can be obtained at www.ICGtesting.com
Printed in the USA
LVOW09s0543141213

365271LV00002BA/3/P